EXCELLER
SELECT
TOP PICKS

Fragments *of an* Unbroken Mirror

Fragments of an Unbroken Mirror

Growing up in a colonial metropolis,
and beyond ...

SANTANU SINHA CHAUDHURI

EXCELLER BOOKS®
A GLOBAL PRESS

Fragments of an Unbroken Mirror
Growing up in a colonial metropolis, and beyond ...

Cover art by Partha Pratim Ghosh
Cover design by Exceller Books
Illustrations by Amit Saha
Author's photograph by Ankit Anand

ISBN: 978-81-19524-19-8

First published in India in 2025 by Exceller Books,
An imprint of GE Group

G1, Dream Apartment, Degree College Road, Belgharia,
Kolkata700056, India
www.excellerbooks.com

EXCELLER BOOKS®
A GLOBAL PRESS

In unfading memory of my parents

Anima (Seba) Sinha and *Sunirmal Sinha Chaudhuri*

I do not know who paints the picture of life on the canvas called memory. Whoever she might be, the process is nothing but painting. That is, she doesn't pick up brushes to make an exact copy of what's happening around her. She casts away lots of things but retains lots of others depending on her whims. Many insignificant events are made bigger and gigantic episodes scaled down. The painter doesn't hesitate to put later things in front and earlier things behind. For a fact, her task is painting pictures, not writing history.

Therefore, on the exterior of our life, there is a procession of events, and within, pictures are painted continuously. The two are connected, but not the same.

Rabindranath Tagore
In the Introduction to his memoirs, *Jeevansmriti*
[Translation by the author]

Foreword

Not many of us would have scores of such true and captivating stories. This book is a surprisingly detailed account of a remarkable childhood and youth lived amid fascinating people and colourful places in and around the city of its author's birth. It's Calcutta in a Capsule. Rarely would you experience a great city through the experiences and memories of numerous people. There are also gloomy glimpses from the past 100 years—the Bengal famine of 1943, refugees from erstwhile East Pakistan, the spread of the Naxalbari movement.

The book sets the scene with a city dweller's imagined double-decker bus ride with all the sights of colonial Calcutta. There's author Santanu's home "anchored on a sea of unmelodious sounds", "beautiful streets smelling of childhood" or the "unpretentious small doors that haven't smelt of new paint for decades"—such evocative imagery weaves through the book. We move on to departed members of the author's family, some "rock-solid" feminine figures, his grandparents or his uniquely eccentric and scholarly uncle, Kaku—witty and moving. We meet ordinary, unremarkable men and women who were unique in their own ways, old friends and their siblings and even friends of friends, a beautiful young girl who may be terminally ill.

This book is also populated with talented people, including great literati and some old masters of the Bengal School of artists from Santiniketan, where Santanu got his BSc in physics. There are brilliant singers and poets we have never heard of, but who come alive through these pages. After about two more years at Santiniketan's Visva-Bharati University, reading for a post-graduate degree, Santanu moved to a career in bank management. Throughout, Santanu Sinha Chaudhuri's storytelling is as clear as an elegant physics equation, yet filled with light adventure, humour, drama and often a poetic pathos. Every chapter, each of the 54 short non-fiction stories here, builds to a subtle climax that made me want to read the next one.

Mohan Sivanand
Artist and former Editor-in-Chief
Reader's Digest, India

Author's Excuses

Truth, Mark Twain famously said, is stranger than fiction. With reverence to the illustrious author, I disagree. I believe the "true facts" of our life are actually not-so-strange yet captivating fiction written in a language that we often fail to read. This book narrates some true anecdotes that you might suspect are fictional.

These stories begin in postcolonial India, a simpler time when technology didn't control our lives, nor did we have the material comforts we often take for granted today. It was a time not far away, yet inconceivably distant. The stories are from my childhood and early youth, that is, from the mid-1950s to the early '70s. The backdrop is a colonial city I grew up in and an atypical campus I was privileged to study at. These of course aren't historical accounts, but as you read the stories, if you get to feel a few heartbeats of the time and its people, I will be happy.

Since the time that cradled these stories, the world has moved from steam engines to interplanetary travel, from manual typewriters to Artificial Intelligence. In general, the changes have been so colossal that sometimes I think my generation was born on a different planet. This memoir chronicles life in an exciting corner of the earth in the beginning of the 70 years during which humans transformed a lot more than what they had in the previous 70,000 years. That fascinating contrast is another theme of this book.

I loved writing the stories. I hope you will enjoy them. Happy reading!

Santanu Sinha Chaudhuri
santanusc@yahoo.com
Bengaluru, 01 November 2024

Contents

Part I: Father of the Man

Part II: The University of Life

Part I
Father of the Man

1| It's Yesterday Once More

In my solitude, I have clearly seen things that are not real.
– Antonio Machado, Spanish poet

This afternoon, when I left my workplace, a bloodless winter sun hung near the horizon behind a veil of fog and dust. I was happy to see the setting sun because the nature of my work being what it is, I didn't get to see an afternoon for months. Until today.

Boys were playing cricket in a corner of the large park on the other side of the road. An ochre blanket of dust kicked up by the cricketers hung over the field around which elderly trees stood like uninterested spectators. The trees, many of them barren and all of them heavy with undisturbed dust of many rainless months, were badly waiting for a winter shower.

The irregularly shaped park, called Park Circus Maidan, is larger than most open spaces in the city, but from a drone flying a few miles above, it would be a tiny speck in a corner of Kolkata, which was Calcutta for long, and the capital of colonial India once. That fact is a tiny speck of history.

For some reason, there was hardly anyone on the road today … almost no vehicles on the carriageways. The men with broken cheeks in shabby grey shirts and short dhotis selling phuchkas at the park entrance had no customers. Although the city has changed inexorably over the past sixty years, neither the taste of the phuchka, nor the appearance of the men who sell them has changed. My friend Jyoti lived near Park Circus Maidan when we were in high school. Jyoti and I spent many an afternoon together in the park, chatting and eyeing up girls, me smoking a secret cigarette and Jyoti—he had all the makings of the abstainer he is today—looking at me disapprovingly. The phuchka sellers, I know each one of them.

* * *

This afternoon, a frosty wind has been blowing since morning; the day is unusually cold. Suddenly, as I was waiting at the bus stop, a mild shiver passed through my spine. The dying daylight seemed unusually dull. The place seemed far too quiet, far too empty, almost surreal. The city looked different in the pale light of the dipping sun. Out of habit, I pulled out my phone to check the time. Surprisingly, there was no signal. In that mysterious twilight at an indeterminable moment, I stood flummoxed on the eerily quiet road.

It was perhaps the perfect setting for a double-decker bus to arrive, the double-decker that had been discarded long ago by officials sitting in air-conditioned offices who had no sense of urban poetry. It was a spanking red Leyland. A majestic monster of a vehicle with the proud head of a Royal Bengal tiger stencilled by the side of its entrance. The double-decker without which the story of my childhood, which I am going to tell you, would be incomplete.

As I climb up the stairs, I find the front seats unoccupied. As a child I loved the front seat on the upper deck, which offered a panoramic view of the city ahead. As our bus moves, as buildings, trees, roads and lampposts march backward, the evening light becomes even mellower, and strangely, the roads become emptier. The two men arguing noisily behind me fall silent. Suddenly, I find all the seats behind me are empty.

A translucent canopy of stillness hangs over the world as the bus takes me along familiar roads and flyovers past familiar structures like the new shopping mall in Amir Ali Avenue, where there was a tram depot once upon a time, the perpetually grey façade of the Modern High School, the green pitch of Calcutta Cricket and Football Club, where football is no longer played. The few pedestrians seem far away. The area looks very unlike the humdrum metropolis I saw hours before. It looks unreal, more like a faded sepia picture stuck with corner hinges in a photo album with thick black pages, an album that was Lost in the Tides of Time long ago.

The bus goes on a journey more in time than in space. The Kolkata of the twenty-first century fades away before my believing eyes and a similar but very different metropolis from a different millennium takes its place.

It's yesterday once more.

2| Childhood Is Home

Saleem Sinai, the protagonist of Salman Rushdie's *Midnight's Children*, was born at the precise moment of India's independence in 1947. On a historical scale, I missed becoming a midnight's child by a whisker. I was born four years after Saleem, less than a decade after a famine killed millions in Bengal, and five years after a horrendous communal riot killed thousands and made partition of India inevitable.

Memories of the famine and the riot were still unhealed wounds in people's mind. For obvious reasons, the riot, which history records as the *Great Calcutta Killings*, was never discussed in the presence of children. However, many a time in my childhood, I heard—most often from my mom—shocking stories of emaciated men, women, and children begging for food and dying uncomplainingly on the footpaths of Calcutta. (Although three to four million people died of starvation, not even one eatery was looted.) Mother never recovered from the memories.

Also, somewhat strangely, I never heard grown-ups discuss what caused the famine. My parents' generation was apparently unaware that the calamity had been manmade. In fact, until 2011, that is, until the publication of Madhusree Mukerjee's *Churchill's Secret War*, while I knew Hitler had killed six million Jews and others with clinical precision, I had no idea that one of the most celebrated Englishmen ever, Winston Churchill was personally responsible for the death of three to four million Indians, who, he anyway considered "a beastly people with a beastly religion".

However, unlike Hitler, Churchill wasn't driven by a craving to kill. The millions who died in the famine of 1942 were collateral damage of efforts to secure food for the Allied soldiers fighting a war on the South Asian theatre and also, an attempt to make life difficult for future invaders, that is, the Indian National Army (INA) led by Subhas Chandra Bose and their Japanese comrades. (Every boat in the riparian districts of Bengal was destroyed, precluding the transport of food grains to many areas.)

As a matter of fact, Churchill's method of mass murder was smarter and more cost-effective. He just cut off all possible supplies of food to Bengal, and that too, shortly after a devastating cyclone ravaged South Bengal and buried the coastal paddy fields under sand. The memories of the famine, the wounds of the Partition, and the deluge of refugees (who had set up rudimentary settlements—we call them *refugee colonies*—around Calcutta) had an invisible but tangible presence in my childhood.

My father's family too had lost their home, but we didn't experience the deprivations of the refugee colonies that I later saw in Ritwik Ghatak's films like *Subarna-Rekha* and *Meghe Dhaka Tara.* We lived in relative comfort on the square top floor of a three-storey building, although my parents struggled to make ends meet. There were six airy and light rooms in our flat and a darkish room at the centre where electric bulbs (with yellow filaments) had to be turned on even in the daytime. But as a small child, I spent much of my daylight hours on the terrace. The large flat terrace gave me a sense of freedom that the city tried to take away.

My parents had married in 1947. Ma's family was from faraway Lower Assam, but her wedding had happened at her uncle's home in Alipore in Calcutta. Baba had migrated to the city long before for college and university education and stayed on in search of a livelihood, in which he was successful intermittently.

In the 1950s, the Bangla word para was significant in city life. Incidentally, to pronounce the word, for both the syllables, we use the vowel sound as in cup or bus, and for the second consonant, a coronal sound that is between /r/ and /d/, which the English language doesn't use.

Conceptually, a pāṛā[1] happens to be a locality or neighbourhood, but these words do not capture the sense of a pāṛā, just as /r/ or /d/ doesn't capture the Bangla consonant sound in between.

In his seminal and controversial book *Sapiens*, Yuval Noah Harari defines *the local intimate community* as a social unit in which people know each other well and more importantly, *depend* on each other for survival. Harari says it has been a part of human society all along. A pāṛā in the colonial metropolis of Calcutta too was an intimate community, which typically consisted of 20 to maybe 50 proximate families that were, in some ways, a single extended family. The entire community would get together on social occasions. Women—only a tiny fraction of them worked outside—would gather on a common terrace every afternoon to share their happiness and sorrow, likings and jealousies, dreams and disappointments. Tattling was an important pastime, criticising people behind their back, a source of pleasure. The activity is captured in a curious English acronym of a Bangla phrase: PNPC: Parō-Nindā-Parō-Charchā (Discussing-Others-Rubbishing-Others).

Boys would fly kites on terraces and play football in the narrow alleys. Separate clusters of men and boys from different age groups would converge on narrow open verandas which were found outside some houses, and solve the problems of the world in lazy evenings and Sunday mornings, aided by sweet milky tea and unfiltered cigarettes. Outside homes, boys and girls lived in separate worlds except during community festivals like the Durga puja. Falling in love would have been a challenging task, stealing a kiss would be nearly impossible. So, love would largely be without a tactile element, as the bard Rabindranath Tagore had written:

Her simple words like a tender touch I find
That weave romantic dreams on my barren mind.

---

[1] To transliterate some Bangla words in this book, including some uncommon place names, I have used the standards of romanisation prescribed in ISO 15919.

As we were the only family that lived in a stand-alone house on a major arterial road of the city, we didn't have the sense of a close-knit locality. My only sibling being an older sister, I was my only playmate in early childhood, until I began going out alone. Our terrace was my playground where I used to score brilliant goals after dodging countless real but non-existent defenders, win many a boxing contest with no one, and fight valiant battles against a dangerous but invisible enemy.

But I wasn't alone really. The building, over fifty years old, had countless cracks and crevices in its unpainted outer walls and the parapet of the terrace. Several colonies of ants that lived in the deep gorges of the wide parapet were my companions. They were of two kinds, small red and large black. I have some shameful memories of an event that happened on the terrace, which I will confess to. Later.

As you climbed down the red stairs from the terrace, you would find my father's office in front—he was self-employed and always worked from home. The room had a large desk behind which stood three elegantly polished glass-fronted wooden bookcases, which created a small anteroom behind. On the other side were two full-length windows looking out to a wide road, along the middle of which clanking trams ran. Dad sat in a revolving chair. Opposite him in two robust chairs, there used to be someone often: a client or friend. The desk had a shiny wooden frame with sloping edges on top; within the frame, there was a covering of Rexine—a material that's seen no more except in Indian railway coaches.

Dad got the Rexine changed from time to time; I recall seeing the table in red, grey, blue, and beige tops. But unlike the colour of the desktop, the story of my father's life never changed. It was the tale of an unending struggle to make a decent living. He spent most of the day sitting behind the desk running whatever business he was in at the moment, and at night, he slept on it.

If you turned left, you would find a longish corridor, on two sides of which were five rooms, three on the right facing the main road and two on the left, separated by a passage. Dad's mother, Snehalata lived in the large room on the left with a full-length window facing the south. The room looked bigger as it had just a cot and an almost bare clotheshorse. All her earthly belongings were kept in a black steel trunk that served as a seat too.

Grandma was a minor enigma.

3| Before the Midnight Struck

It seems it is mandatory for humans to search for their roots.[i] –
Mihir Sengupta

There is always a beginning before the beginning, an evening before the midnight. Until the Partition of India, our family lived in a village called Rāḍhishāl in the northeastern corner of what is now Bangladesh. As a child, I heard from my father that fourteen generations of his forefathers had lived in the same place. The expression "fourteen generations" is an idiom in Bangla, which means a very long period of time in the genealogy of a family. But my father didn't use the phrase metaphorically; he actually meant fourteen generations; he could reel out the names of his fourteen forefathers.

In Bengal, Rāḍh refers to the largely arid land on the west bank of the Hooghly; it includes what are presently the districts of Bardhaman, Birbhum, Bankura, Purulia, and a part of Hooghly in West Bengal. According to the oral history passed on through generations in our family, one of our forefathers had to leave his home in Rāḍh and set up a village in the rain-drenched district of Sylhet, which was far away from whoever (or whatever) was troubling him. Sylhet was also protected by a tangle of rivers. The name of our village, Rāḍhishāl points at our family's past home in Rāḍh, which is now buried in oblivion. Our first surname Sinha seems to be a corruption of Singh, a common surname in North India, and it perhaps carries a hint of a much longer migration.

If a generation equals 25 years, Rāḍhishāl would have been set up sometime in the second half of the sixteenth century, when Akbar was the emperor in Delhi (1556-1605). Later, in British India, our family was a part of the Indian ruling class at its lowest rung. Our family used to pay taxes directly to the colonial government, and hence were called zamindars.

Zamindars had quite a lot of power in their fiefdoms as long as they managed to pay taxes to the Crown. But thanks to the Permanent Settlement Act of 1793, also known as the Sunset Act, the threat of losing zamindari hung over their heads at all times. If they failed to pay the contracted tax to the government treasury by a fixed date every year, his estate would be put to auction. Period.

The story goes that once, my grandpa's grandpa faced the prospect of losing his estate as tax collections had been poor that year. As he smoked hookah sitting under a tree, a hanger-on suggested, 'Sir! "..." has made it big as a cloth merchant. Why don't you get your second son married to his daughter?'

The dowry was big enough to cover the unpaid taxes. The story points at two social realities. First, the iron-clad caste system could be broken if it was to the advantage of the upper caste. In the normal course, a man from a family that belonged to the landed gentry wouldn't marry a trader's daughter. But he might, if it suited him, or if he had taken a fancy in a girl/woman from a "lower caste". (It had the sanction of the hypocritical Hindu code of ethics too, which said a man could marry a woman from the lower caste; such marriages were sanctified as "anulom" marriage. However, the reverse was a taboo.)

The second indication is that we were not wealthy, something that fits with what I heard about the financial standing of my forefathers. In public perception, the word zamindar is associated with opulence. In a time in India when prostitution was a part of culture, a zamindar was supposed to live in a mansion, maintain a few concubines elsewhere and generally make merry, with dancing women lighting up his court under chandeliers while the man himself was surrounded by sycophants, drinking. Thanks to numerous films—not the least of which is Satyajit Ray's *Jalsaghar*—this picture of a zamindar has been etched in stone in our mind. Also, many zamindars were at the forefront of spreading education. Many of the schools and colleges in rural Bengal were set up by generous landowners.

Neither of the two contrasting descriptions, that is, of the idle, splurging rich or the well-heeled trailblazer of the society matches our family's past. Our family lived in mud houses and apart from a large pond and a common shed for conducting Durga Puja every year, they had no trappings of wealth. But they did have some trappings of power. They referred to villagers as prajā, that is, "subjects", who would bow down and stand aside when they met someone from the landlord's family on the road. Even elderly villagers would address little boys of the family using the deferential form of you in Bangla, āpni (āfnē, in our dialect). Also, the family had a small band of lathi-wielding men to deal with recalcitrant "subjects".

A part of the village was reserved for the family; no one else could build homes there. However, a midwife and another man called Nadiabasi, a maid's son, lived in the privileged area. The midwife perhaps had earned her position of honour because most family children had been brought to the world by her. But what about the maid's son Nadiabasi, who even used tumi, the non-deferential you to address family members? I will answer the question in a moment.

My grandfather had an older and two younger brothers. The older brother Kshetramohan, a bachelor, was the family patriarch, who—from all available accounts—was mean, cantankerous, and much unloved. However, he apparently had no major vices except smoking cannabis. Nadiabasi, slightly older than Kshetramohan, would address the latter by his first name and was the only person who would dare to criticise him openly. The maid's offspring could do so because he was an illegitimate older half-brother of Kshetramohan. A Vidura in the family, he too was sagacious and widely respected.

Kshetramohan's younger brother, my grandfather Lalitmohan lived with grandma and their three children in a rented house in the nearby town of Hōbiganj—eight miles away from our village—so that his children could attend school. From what I heard from my father, grandpa was a principled man with a serious OCD, who brought up his children under strict rules. He would force his sons to do housework, including cleaning cowsheds, something that wasn't common practice for people from his station in life. Grandpa also washed coins before he touched them! Ironically, despite such serious efforts to ward off diseases, he died in his thirties.

Lalitmohan was qualified to practise in the local court, which would have been one of the lowest law courts of the British Raj; but he didn't join the legal profession apparently because he refused to tell lies. Unfortunately, his truthfulness was never seriously tested as he could run his family with what he earned from his estate as a lesser absentee landlord. But it can be safely said that he was not keen on making money, a trait that still runs in the family, besides OCD!

Grandpa Lalitmohan married Snehalata from the family of Nandi Majumdars from Bejura in the same district. Grandma apparently came from a more enlightened family than her husband's. An aunt of hers was a qualified doctor, one of the first "lady doctors" in undivided Bengal. She used to travel in palanquins and bullock carts to distant villages to treat women in distress. I do not know her name as Father always referred to her as "Doctor Dida". Doctor Grandma, it seems, had a fine sense of humour.

Those days, lottery tickets were sold by name; the winners' names would be published in newspapers. One day, great-granny asked my dad, who was a child then, 'Please check if my name is on the list.'

Dad did, and told her it wasn't there. But she didn't trust him, 'I think you haven't learned how to read well. Read again.'

Dad did. But she was still not satisfied. She made her grandnephew read the list once more. Then she said with a sigh of relief, 'Good that I didn't buy a ticket!'

On another occasion, she said, 'You people make such an uproar about Tagore and Gandhi. Ha! I am greater than both.'

'How?!' Her grandnieces and-nephews exclaimed.

'Well, my handwriting is better than Gandhi's.'

'And Tagore?'

'I am older.'

* * *

When his old man died, my father was 11. He had a brother two years younger and a little sister. The brothers had traditional names: Ramkrishna and Ramgopal. My aunt's name was old-fashioned even by the standards of the time, Kalitara.

After her husband's death, grandma Snehalata continued to live in Hobigunj, presumably for continued schooling of her offspring. But the family purse strings were controlled by a tight-fisted Kshetramohan. Snehalata and her children struggled to make ends meet apparently for no good reason.

Decades after Father's passing, I travelled from Hōbiganj to "our village" by a comfortable Toyota taxi. On the way, we crossed a river with a familiar name, Sutān, and a few other streams. As we drove through the flat plain of golden paddy fields, daylight was fading. It seemed apart from the well-maintained bitumen roads, the imported Toyota, and the rattling steel bridges, nothing much had changed since my father's time. Didn't see electric posts. Brick-and-mortar houses were rare.

I tried to visualise a boy walking the distance of eight miles on slushy paths from Hōbiganj to Rāḍhishāl to plead for money for his school fees that hadn't arrived. The success of Ramkrishna's mission depended on Kshetramohan's moods. Many a time, the boy came back emptyhanded, to try again the following Sunday. He didn't mind the physical effort, but the humiliation of being a supplicant hurt.

Apart from educating himself and worrying about money, the two preoccupations that would never leave him, even before completing school, my father did something quite precocious. He got his name and the names of his siblings changed: Ramkrishna became Sunirmal, Ramgopal became Subimal, and Kalitara, Anima. My aunt in particular was hugely grateful to her older bro for rechristening her. Kalitara would have been a most incongruous name for a fashionable English-spouting business executive with short hair and red lipstick.

Can you imagine the archetypal urbane lover boy of Indian cinema, Dev Anand as Dharamdev Pishorimal Anand?

4|One Family, Two Nations

'Can you ever divide a country just like that? Is it an ash gourd or radish that you can cut into two?' Grandpa would look at pouring rains. 'Rainwaters will wash away the border between the two nations.' As he kept looking at the rains, his eyes grew cataract; the two countries didn't become one.[ii]

– Kallol Lahiri

Grandma Snehalata, thakuma to me, was a thin, dark, toothless, bespectacled woman in her fifties. She always wore white and smiled rarely. Maybe, all her smiles had dried up when she was widowed in her twenties. Bringing up three children without a husband and with a tenuous, meagre income from the medium-sized family farmlands in a remote corner of India bled white by colonial rule couldn't have been easy. But although she was rather morose, difficulties in life hadn't made her bitter. She was at peace with herself and exceedingly fond of me. And although she never cuddled or kissed me—in fact, she never said a word of affection—I knew I was a central piece among the few building blocks that remained in her life.

Grandma was a singularly calm person who talked in a small voice and seldom spoke, qualities that were not inherited by any of her three offspring, Dad, his younger brother, or sister. Thakuma used to read Bangla books and magazines through the day till she went completely blind after a failed cataract surgery, which was not uncommon those days. Then she would beg my sister Ruby and me to read aloud to her. I rarely obliged; Ruby did, often.

I suspect grandma was somewhat irreligious. Unlike other Hindu women of her time, offering puja to a brood of deities kept in a corner of her bedroom or elsewhere was not her principal activity, although I believe she would have offered her prayers at times. But importantly, she had no idols in her room; they had been assigned to my mom. However, Snehalata often talked adoringly about the deity Shyam Sundar back home in the family temple, who she perhaps had had a secret affair with. Shyam Sundar incidentally is one of the 108 names of Krishna, a major deity and a flamboyant character in the Hindu pantheon who happened to be a ladies' man.

Like all middle-class Bengali Hindu widows of her time, she cooked her solitary vegetarian meal of the day herself—in her bedroom—over a portable coal-fired oven in the late morning. While she ate, I hung around like a cat. She would happily share her frugal meal with me. Even today, I can close my eyes and feel the heavenly taste of her spice-free curries cooked in drops of oil. But for some reason, my only sibling, Ruby was never a part of the mid-day meal scheme. I didn't think of it then, but as a child I knew that grandma was brazenly partial to me. Incidentally, my mother too, like her mom-in-law, leaned heavily towards the male child.

But unlike other mothers-in-law, Snehalata did not try to control my mother's life. Ma too, apart from covering her head casually in the older woman's presence, did nothing special to please her. In fact, she never made any attempt to look deferential when grandma was around. Thakuma's relationship with Ma was similar to her attachment to the rest of the world, standoffish, but always peaceful. Her attitude to life was seen while we played ludo, a board game for two to four, in which each player has four tiny plastic tokens to move along a set of squares based on the numbers thrown up by a dice. The fun part of the game lay in "killing" opponent's tokens when luck and a little guile led you to the square where the opponent's tile had already been.

But Thakuma would never kill and expect us to return the favour. She would say in Sylheti, 'You don't kill mine; I won't kill yours.'

She would often travel to our ancestral home, the village called Rāḍhishāl in East Pakistan. To reach home, Snehalata would fly to Agartala by an Indian Airlines' Dakota and from there, cross the international border by a cycle rickshaw. While returning, she would carry exotic homemade sweets that also looked exquisite as they had been cast in earthen/wooden dies with intricate designs. We looked forward to her return because her steel trunk contained, besides sweets and her meagre belongings of a few white saris and underclothing, a jackfruit wrapped in newspaper from our "own" tree that had ceased to be our own.

We had to eat the jackfruit quickly as our home had no refrigerator. Food used to be preserved in a meat safe, that is, a wooden cupboard with wire mesh on three sides for air circulation. When grandma had her siesta, I would desperately steal from her treasure trove of sweets kept in the meat safe or elsewhere. She used to hide the sweets as well as she could, but being a smart kid, I could always find them out.

Little did I know that what I used to discover after much toil was only a red herring. She would keep a few pieces at a discoverable place, but her main stock would be safely hidden elsewhere.

5| Grandpa Calling?

I have written that my old man's father died when his children were little. My mother's dad too died before I was born. Actually, a few months before.

I have no idea how my grandpa on Dad's side looked, because although he died long after photography was invented (1827, Mr Google tells me), it was long before the technology reached rural Bengal. However, I can clearly see my mom's dad if I close my eyes. In a moment, I'll tell you how, but before that, let me take you back to a remote village on the eastern fringe of undivided Bengal in the early 20th century.

In the evening of his wedding, my mother's father, Tara Bhushan Pal was in his soon-to-be father-in-law's home. Astrologers had decided that the wedding should happen late in the night. As the evening grew old, most invitees left, it was pitch dark beyond the circle of dazzling glow of the Petromax lamps. Shortly before the priests were to begin their work, Tara Bhushan came to know that without his knowledge but on his behalf, a fat dowry had been cadged out from the bride's father by his oldest brother, who was much older than him and the head of the family. Calling him aside, Tara Bhushan said the wedding could happen only if the dowry was returned.

In 1911, such an act was almost revolutionary because of two reasons. First, it was long before dowry was considered a social evil; it was the "done thing" or "SOP", depending on your lexical preference. Rabindranath Tagore, the doyen of Bangla literature and a great social reformer, wrote many stories on the evils of dowry although he himself had given dowry to his sons-in-law, at least one of whom turned out to be a scoundrel. Second, a younger sibling overruling an older, that too, the head of the family, would have been like a bloody mutiny in those feudal times.

Tara Bhushan moved to Karimgunj, a sub-divisional head-quarters on the banks of the river Kushiara in Sylhet, where he set up a legal practice. Over time, Tara Bhushan became a highly respected lawyer. Karimgunj is the only place in the world which has a road named after someone from my family.

Also, he and his wife Sushama Pal had quite a brood: four sons and four daughters. Then my grandma died at the age of 37 of complications related to frequent child bearing. But Tara Bhushan didn't marry again, which too was unusual in his time and place.

I am inclined to believe it showed his devotion to the departed wife, but that's just a guess. What is beyond debate is that he brought up his seven children single-handed on top of his demanding legal practice. (One died young in an accident.) And from the stories I heard from Ma, he was exceedingly affectionate towards his offspring. Both a father and mother to them.

* * *

As I have said, Tara Bhushan died months before I was born. Sometimes, Mother indulged herself in the fantasy that her father had come back in my shape. But the hypothesis was weak because temperamentally, I was very different from my grandpa. Whenever I got angry, whenever I threw tantrums, my mom reflected—with deep sadness—that her only son hadn't inherited the even temper of her father.

Tara Bhushan died with the standing that he had never ever lost his cool. And I think the reputation was not unfounded when I think of my cousins Arindam, Chandan, and Monica, who too carry 25% of Tara Bhushan's genes. They are all pretty much unflappable.

Mother had a framed six-by-eight black-and-white photo of Tara Bhushan. It showed an elderly man in his mid-sixties smiling pleasantly at you. That means the picture would have been taken when grandpa was about as old as I am now, as I write his story.

Mom always placed the photo at a place where she could see him when she woke up in the morning. She would begin the day with a pranam to her departed father; she would carry the picture along even when she went on holidays. Over five decades, almost every day I saw Tara Bhushan Pal, a successful small-town lawyer, a kindly single parent, and a principled man much ahead of his time. Consequently, his physiognomy got firmly etched in my head. Then my mother died and the framed portrait lost its pride of place. That happened 20 years ago and I have no idea where it is now.

That is how human beings actually die, slowly, imperceptibly, as their memories fade. These days, grandpa rarely crosses my mind.

This morning, as I got up and stood before the bathroom mirror with a toothbrush in hand, I was shocked.

Tara Bhushan Pal was looking at me benignly from the other side of the mirror.

Genes! What tricks they play!

6| Love and Care

Each one treasured his childhood memories like a title deed.[iii]
– William Dalrymple

Mother began teaching at a girls' school, Victoria Institution, when I was an infant. She would leave by nine in the morning and return in the evening. I used to sleep with one of her used saris, soaking in the mamma smell. Sudha, a dark young woman with a chiselled face and a shock of long black curly hair, looked after my sister and me. We called her by adding the suffix -di to her name. One of my earliest memories is Sudhadi telling bizarre stories and feeding me. It wouldn't have been easy to make me eat. Sudhadi would make a ball with rice and curry and say, 'This is a quail's egg. Better eat quickly, or else, a crow is waiting on the windowsill.'

Then she said 'Whoosh!', and with simultaneous swings of two arms, shooed away the phantom crow and put the ball of rice delicately into my mouth. The act would be repeated, with a pigeon's egg, a swan's egg, and so on …

Sudhadi stopped working with us when I had grown up a little, but she would drop in often. I followed her journey through life as her raven-black hair turned salt-and-pepper and then silver. But not much else changed in her. She had no offspring. And she treated me as her only child. She called me by a name that no one else used. The special name perhaps symbolised the special relationship I shared with her. The bond remained intact till her death.

Her husband, Rajen, who sister and I called Rajenda, was a jack of many trades. He assisted my father in diverse ways from working as a watchman to keeping accounts. Earlier, Rajenda had earned his living by painting hoardings. An accidental fall from a scaffolding and a few broken bones here and there had forced him to go through the ignominy of the life of an odd-jobber. But a singularly cheerful person, he never showed any sign of regret.

Rajenda, who loved reading, also had several quirky habits. For example, when I began exploring the world outside and went to their ten-by-ten-feet one-room home in a slum, there was a huge stack of copies of *Betar Jagat (The Wireless World)*, the fortnightly bulletin of All India Radio. An avid radio listener, Rajenda apparently had every copy of Betar Jagat since its inception. When I asked him why he was collecting them all, he replied, 'Someday, they won't find their old copies and declare a big prize for the collector who had them all. Wait and see, I will make a fortune from my Betar Jagats.'

Rajenda didn't make his fortune but listening to radio regularly had made him and a well-informed man an accomplished speaker. He had a natural wit and he modulated his voice for the precise effect. And like any good speaker, he would pause a moment before delivering his punch line. Also, he could recite beautifully serious long poems of Rabindranath Tagore from memory.

Rajenda was a friend, ally, and mentor of a lonely child. I will come back to him later.

Besides my parents, grandma, and older sister Ruby, dad's younger sister Anima, who worked as a clerk at a central government office, lived with us until her marriage. Recently, in some context, a friend has written: An "enterprising Bengali" is an oxymoron like, say, "India Made Foreign Liquor". My aunt was a rare specimen of an enterprising Bengali. After much manoeuvring in the bureaucracy, including cadging a little help from a distant relative who was a big shot in the corridors of power in New Delhi, she managed to get herself posted at the Indian Embassy in London. (As a child, I was unaware of how she had gone to London; much later after her passing, I found a moth-eaten file in our attic which chronicled her efforts.) She had been married when she went to London. There, she acquired a coveted professional qualification, studying in the evening for several years. After return, she parked herself at a much higher level professionally in a leading private company. Aunt was much more than an aunt. She was like another mother to Ruby and me. I was four when she got married and Bhabani Kaku, a prosperous Assamese businessman in the tea industry, became our Pishemoshai.

But until her marriage, there was some tension between my dad on one side and the allied forces of Aunt and grandma on the other. Just as Switzerland didn't join either of the sides in the two World Wars, mom took a strictly neutral position during the occasional family scraps. Consequently, she was unpopular with both sides.

I now feel that the reasons for the family discords were mostly financial. My father, a small businessman, didn't have a steady income. In fact, he was a square peg in a round hole in the world of business. But he pegged away all the same. Repeated failures didn't frustrate him, just as occasional successes didn't elate him.

My mom's tiny salary as a school teacher steadied the boat somewhat, but the glass was never full. When we went to buy clothes, Ma would size up a frock for Ruby and a shirt and pair of shorts for me. We would try them on and look prim in our snugly fitting clothes. Then Ma would tell the store assistant, 'Give the same things, but two sizes larger.'

Consequently, neither Ruby nor I have a photograph where the frock or the shorts don't extend well below our knees. One of the main attractions of Durga Puja was that we would get a pair of new shoes. (Fortunately, those were never oversized!) Boyhood of my generation would be incomplete without Naughty-Boy shoes from Bata. They had circular toes and would refuse to be torn despite ruthless torture including serving as football boots almost every day. They had better survive a year. We would be entitled to another pair only before the next Durga Puja.

Most children used discarded stuff as playthings. There would be few among my friends who wouldn't have experienced the joy of making a telephone out of two matchbox trays and a piece of string. An older cousin Nandan, when he was in Calcutta, and I flew planes from the cockpit of our attic, using controls consisting of a few broken electrical switches, a fan regulator without its insulation cover but with a lever that made an astonishingly loud noise for its size when it was shifted from one contact point to another. The most fascinating object of course was a discarded car gear shaft which had somehow found its way into our car-less home. It served as the joystick.

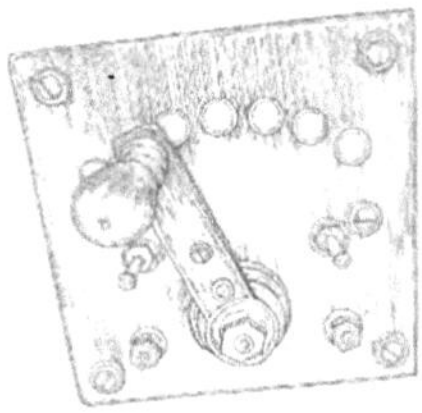

Almost any piece of wood served as a cricket bat; a real bat was an unimaginable luxury. In my entire early childhood, the most memorable toys I had were a few engineering sets which had the brand name "Meccano" with pieces that could be assembled into lots of things from handcarts to suspension bridges using nuts and bolts supplied in the kit.

But by far the most fanciful toy I got was from Aunt: a to-scale die-cast six-inch red London double-decker bus. It was a perfect replica, with seats and stairs made of yellowish plastic. What I found most fascinating about it was the vertical steel post at the entrance. I would play with it for hours, but treated it with the respect it deserved. I often dreamed of my double-decker. I guess it was the same double-decker I would board many decades later in a bleak winter afternoon.

One day, a family who had a boy smaller than me visited us. I do not remember if he made a fuss about the bus, but my parents asked me to give it to him. I obliged. I felt bad, but it was okay. Or was it? Our life is a story of acquiring and losing objects and people we love and clearly, that particular loss was big enough not to be forgotten.

The number and quality of toys urban middle-class children have these days is a good pointer to how well the "great Indian middle class" has done in the last half a century. I often feel bad for the kids today. Poor things would not know the divine joy of getting a new toy after dreaming about it for years!

7|A Face in the Crowd

Simplicity is the ultimate sophistication.
– Leonardo da Vinci

We lived three buildings away from a major crossing in South Calcutta, in an area teeming with people of different shapes, sizes, complexions, and clothing. Among the images from my childhood that have been etched forever in my mind, one was an elderly man who sold newspapers in front of our house in the morning mainly to the occupants of passing cars.

He was tall, lean, and straight. He would turn himself out in a suit in every season, and a hat to complete the authentic European attire. But if you watched him carefully, you would see his clothes were ragged and torn and his hat was frayed. He used to sell only English newspapers to the passers-by and exhort them to buy papers in his bass voice. His English was as impeccable as the cut of his jacket: "*The Statesman* Sir, please check what's happening on the Indo-China border. Are the Chinese going to invade India?" And so on.

In a Bangla novel written by Shankar, *Knowing the Unknown (Katō Ajānārē)*, there is a story about a brilliant lawyer who had studied law in England and began practising in Calcutta High Court when the city was the commercial hub of the country. Everyone expected him to reach the pinnacle of his profession along with the comforts of a wealthy lifestyle. But somewhere down the road, the script changed. Through a succession of mishaps, the prospective top barrister ended up a pauper. But in all his defeats, he never lost his self-esteem. He would always be impeccably turned out; he conducted himself with a haughty dignity that had been a part of himself. After growing up, when I read the novel, the image of the suited newspaper vendor at Hazra Crossing flashed through my mind. Could he have been the failed hero in Shankar's story?

One could look at the suited man from two contrary viewpoints: with the mushy sentimentality of Shankar, or as a caricature of a brown sahib who had failed to recognise that his colonial masters had been swept away by the tides of history. If you shared the second perspective, you could perhaps consider him an alter ego of Nirad C Chaudhuri, albeit at the other end of the spectrum, a complete and devastating failure.

* * *

There was a cinema named Basusree flash opposite our house. It was an important part of the landscape and it will return to my story. I saw my first movie there: V. Santharam's *Do Aankhe Barah Haath.* Although I knew no Hindi, I could more or less follow the story of the jailor and the six surly murderers he reformed, but the unforgettable Lata Mangeshkar song *Aye Maalik Tere Bande Hum* did not register in my mind then. In the film, the hard work of the men and their mentor produced a rich harvest. Towards the end, when the six reformed men were being beaten up by villagers who had been threatened by their enterprise, I cried bitterly.

Naturally, I didn't know then that the film was based on the true story of a Gandhian experiment, but those two hours left an imprint on the rest my life. Our personality is shaped by the families we are born in, the schools we attend, and our life experiences in general, but bits and pieces like the two hours of watching *Do Aankhe* … in early childhood too leave indelible marks on us.

While we are talking about films, I can perhaps tell you that of the many business ventures that my father set up and shut down, one was painting film hoardings and other signs. Posters in front of theatres and also, film "posters-on-wheels" were all painted by hand on large canvas sheets. The technology for printing large banners was yet to arrive. Incidentally, most of these paintings could put photographs to shame. Rajenda, who I have written about earlier, met Baba as a painter of hoardings, but I think he didn't paint images; he just painted the letters. But all these had happened when I was an infant, or maybe, even earlier. I have no recollection of the undertaking. But I heard later that some upcoming film stars would come to the tiny room on our terrace (which would serve as the cockpit of my aircraft later) to watch their pictures being painted. Uttam Kumar, a future heart-throb of millions and the supreme Bengali matinee idol of the twentieth century, was one of them.

The person who told me the story was Subhash Kar, who my sister and I called Subhash Kaku. (Kaku stands for an uncle on the father's side). Subhashh Kar was an antithesis of Uttam Kumar: neither fair nor dark, of unremarkable height, and prematurely balding. In Bangla, Subhash means someone who talks softly. True to his name, he was a quiet, soft-spoken person. There was such an air of humility about him … if you met him, you would feel he felt guilty and apologetic all the time, as if he had sneaked into a party uninvited, as if he had no right to be anywhere.

He too had met my father as a painter of hoardings. He didn't leave us when the studio was shut down because by then, he had become a part of the family. He had graduated in painting at the Government Art College, Calcutta and his principal source of income was tutoring children in painting.

Unfortunately for Subhash Kaku, he was born in a time when the commercial aspect of fine arts was yet to be discovered by the likes of MF Hussain, Satish Gujral, or Jogen Chowdhury. Those days, fine art as profession unfailingly led one to poverty. Two nephews of poet Rabindranath Tagore, Gaganendranath and Abanindranath, were painters. Just as Claude Monet, Édouard Manet, Edger Degas, and others had broken the rubrics of classical painting and founded the Impressionist School in France in the nineteenth century, Abanindranath and his brother established the Bengal School of Painting in the early twentieth century to reinvent traditional Indian painting in the modern context. Artists extraordinaire, they belonged to one of the richest families of Bengal. But finally, the great painters had to sell their residential mansion to pay off debts[iv].

With regard to style, Subhash Kar belonged to the Bengal School and in terms of financial standing, he followed his gurus diligently. Subhash Kaku also played the flute and needless to say, it didn't improve his financial situation one jot. He was always in a dhoti and a shabby grey shirt that was well past its use-by date. He smiled an innocent, childlike smile all the time.

The ever-smiling Subhash Kaku was my father's Man Friday. Subhash also had a reputation of botching up things occasionally and I suspect Baba used to give him an earful at times. However, it was also obvious that the older man treated the younger one with a lot of affection; he just couldn't do without Subhas. Subhash Kaku's respect for Baba was enormous, and it wasn't unmixed with fear.

Subhash Kaku, who stayed alone, never spoke of his family. Possibly, he was an estranged child of a family well-established in Santiniketan, a place famous for the experimental school set up by Rabindranath Tagore. Once—when I was very small—he accompanied our family to a weekend tour to Santiniketan. I still have sepia memories of that distant visit. I remember a simple small house surrounded by countless trees and a wall hanging with an exquisite design. I'll come back to Santiniketan in this memoir.

A basic difference between an adult and a child is that a child never tries to mend others' ways. Subhash Kaku never tried to make Ruby and me well-behaved children. He was the only grown-up person in our childhood who would treat us as equals, not as kids. Only true artists can deal with children with such simplicity. Subhash Kaku was an eternal child at heart who had a few things in common with us siblings.

For one, he was as scared of father as we were. For another, mother loved him almost the way she loved us, and would often protect him from her short-tempered husband. Ma often recited these lines from Tagore:

So many homes you've put me in,
Made me know the unknown,
You've brought the distant close, my friend,
And made strangers my own.

Much later, Subhash Kaku found a job as a school teacher, married, and rented a house at Baruipur, which was an hour by train from the city. Problems continued to dog him. His daughter was born with a heart condition that required a series of complex and risky surgeries. He would visit us regularly and was with us in happiness and sorrow for five decades.

When my mother was terminally ill, he too had become frail. He could no longer visit us but would telephone regularly and write postcards to enquire after Boudi. I wrote back to him from time to time, but could not phone him as he didn't have a telephone. When my mother died in 2001, I wrote to him.

The inland letter came back with the note "addressee left". I believe the addressee had left for a place where there are no public telephone booths and where postcards aren't sold.

During the fifty years I knew him, I never saw Subhash Kaku without a smile. Neither did I ever hear him complain about anything. He was a rare contented soul.

Without knowing, he taught me something: Happiness doesn't depend on things that happen to or around me. It depends just on me.

Why have I forgotten the lesson so often?

8| A Colourful Neighbourhood

Prior to the Industrial Revolution, the daily life of most humans ran its course within three ancient frames: the nuclear family, the extended family and the local intimate community. (An 'intimate community' is a group of people who know each other well and depend on each other for survival.)

– Yuval Noah Harari[V]

Similarity between different parts of a planned city is often tiresome. But an organically grown city has many diverse facets. The Calcutta of my childhood looked very different as you moved from one area to another. The downtown Esplanade or Park Street had wide roads, freshly painted office buildings, glamorous stores, restaurants, and bars. As you moved towards the periphery, the roads became narrower, the buildings smaller and mostly, without a fresh coat of paint. The last bit was a little incongruous as Calcutta produced much of the paint used in the country; leading paint manufacturers, Shalimar, British Paints, and ICI had their corporate offices in the city and plants nearby. In a way, the city seemed to be like the man who lit gas lights in her streets, who, the poet Sukanta Bhattacharya imagined, had no means to light a lamp in his own home.

Moving back to diversity, the southern part of the city, which came up later, was swankier. North Calcutta, with its narrow lanes crammed with old edifices looked strange to my eyes.

Once I accompanied Mother to a ground-floor home in a narrow alley in the north as the sun was setting. In the eerily quiet neighbourhood, coal-fired stoves had just been lit in every home. Soon, white smoke covered the locality. It was difficult to breathe, but the scene was breathtaking: old, decaying, closely packed buildings on either side of a narrow lane floating in a white cloud that filtered in the twilight. I wish I could paint the cityscape.

But the evenings near our house were different. Apart Basusree opposite our house, there were four cinemas nearby. That made our locality more crowded and less quiet than most other parts of the city. The cinemas had large, brightly-lit hoardings on their façade. At dusk, the absence of daylight was hardly felt. Just before six in the evening, as the matinee was over, a sea of humanity came out of the hall and crashed on the wave of people trying to get in. The scene would be accompanied by a shrill noise as the men selling small eats shouted themselves hoarse.

Some young louts earned their daily bread, or maybe, a part of their daily bread, by "black-marketing" movie tickets near the cinema. ("Black marketing" is the pan-India verb for an age-old trading practice where sellers create an artificial scarcity of a product and sell it at an inflated price.) When the theatre in front of our house began showing a new film, there would be even more noise in the area and stage whispers of "Do ka paanch!" would be heard above the din. Those guys have vanished. Nowadays, legal tickets cost far more than what those goons would have charged their clients, even after correcting for inflation.

The pavements on either side of the road in front of our house had evergreen conical deodar trees that would be hacked down during the construction of the Calcutta Metro in the 1980s. At one of the four corners of the crossing near our house, there was a lovely little park with lots of trees and a small manicured garden.

In the afternoon, Sudhadi would take Ruby and me to the park. A charming girl, Tata, and her younger sister were our best friends. As the sun went down, the shadow cast by the houses on the west gobbled up the entire park and darkness deepened. Sudhadi cajoled us to return home, but I desperately tried to extend our outing, while my sister, more law-abiding, would be ready to oblige. At that moment, a man would arrive with a burning flame tied to the end of a pole. With a deft move, he would open the glass door of the lampposts in the park, turn on the gas, and ignite the stream of gas. By then, gaslights had been replaced by electric streetlights on the main roads. But fortunately, in the park, the magical spectacle of the gas light being lit happened every evening. I desperately waited for the moment.

Diagonally opposite the park was an imposing L-shaped five-storey building. It had a rounded façade along its two outer sides

and a wide portico supported by broad columns all along. (The portico is gone now as the roads have been widened.) While families lived on the upper floors of the five-storey building which had no lift, about a hundred people slept under its portico at night.

During the day, a medley of commerce happened on the ground and first floors of the building: from a bank to a railway office to a man selling syrupy sherbet from a tiny strip of a shop. On his counter was an array of bottles containing enticingly colourful liquids. He had no fridge to offer his customers a cold drink. During summer, on the dirty unwashed footpath in front of his store, the sherbet man would crush a large chunk of ice in a wet canvas bag by hammering it with a wooden club. The asymmetrically broken pieces of ice would go into the sherbet to offer pleasure and bacteria to the people who drank it. Hygiene was obviously not high on his agenda, but none of his customers was reported to be dead by poisoning.

Under the portico of the building, dozens of men and boys earned their living by offering a range of services from typewriting to polishing shoes. The shoeshine boys made a continuous rat-tat-tat by hitting their wooden box with the rear side of their brush.

The most striking individual among the workmen was a stout, dark, dignified, elderly gentleman who sat on a wooden stool and sold newspapers and magazines. Everyone called him Master Moshai because he had been a schoolteacher in East Bengal before 1947. I cannot say why I liked him, but he did impress me with his quiet dignity. Clearly, Master Moshai just managed to eke out a living. Life would have treated him harshly. Once I too did.

I bought magazines from him occasionally. Once, Master Moshai borrowed a few rupees from me. When he failed to repay on the promised day and for some time thereafter, I harassed him relentlessly. The elderly gentleman looked pitiable, but I showed no mercy. I was perhaps as ruthless as the Pathan money-lenders who lived nearby and whose story I am going to tell you soon. For that sin, I was condemned to work as a banker later in my life.

Beside our house, there was a petrol station. The absence of a tall building allowed a cold breeze to blow in from the south in sultry summer evenings. My sister and I loved to sit down by the full-length windows and play ludo with our grandma. It was the opposite equivalent of sitting by a fireplace in a cold country.

The owner of the petrol station was an elderly Sardarji who had a flowing, long white beard and a Ford T-20 convertible. Occasionally, he would drive down to the place towards the evenings and sit down with his friends at a corner. The Sikh group laughed often and apparently enjoyed every moment of their loud gup-shup in a language we didn't follow. At times, but not always, they had glasses of some mysterious amber liquid in their hands.

9| From Petrol Station to Human Neighbours

The tradition lives on.

As I have said, we lived in a stand-alone house surrounded by stores and small businesses. We didn't have much sense of a neighbourhood or what Yuval Noah Harari called *the local intimate community*. But it is not that we didn't have neighbours.

Our bedroom was on the east. As sunlight used to stream in through two large windows, we were forced to become early risers. Behind our three-storey building lived a family in a house with a fairly large garden and several cottages with corrugated tin roofs. Their jackfruit tree was right under our bedroom window. The family consisted of elderly parents, one grown-up son and several sisters who were much older than Ruby and me. We called the sisters by adding to their names pishi, which in Bangla means an aunt on the father's side. The oldest among them was Lata Pishi, who my sister and I were particularly fond of.

Theirs was a religious family that regularly organised singing of hymns in praise of Lord Krishna. In keertans, the refrain *Hare Krishna, Hare Krishna, Krishna Krishna, Hare Hare* came back again and again in chorus through the day. There was little variation in the tune or the words, which induced sleep in children but took believing adults into a trance.

No Bengali festival can happen without a community meal. For this reason, my slightly older sister Ruby and I looked forward to the festivals in Lata Pishi's house. Holi was the occasion when the biggest gathering and longest keertans took place. This deeply religious and happy family had their moments of trial. One night, we were awakened by loud wails from the house. Lata Pishi's father had passed away suddenly. I remember the night because it was my first brush with death. Baba put on his trademark white khadi dhoti and kurta in the middle of the night and went to their house. And I think Ma too didn't sleep that night.

Over time, all the sisters of Lata Pishi got married and left. Her brother died young. But she lived happily there, with her widowed sister-in-law. We kept visiting each other and much later, my daughter and son got the same affection from her that my sister and me got as kids. Lata Pishi is a remarkably capable woman who ran her business, a coal and kerosene depot, with seeming ease. She adopted a Nepali boy, who took over the responsibility of running her business in due course. Foster mother, adopted son, and foster aunt lived happily ever after. Can you guess what Lata Pishi calls her son? No prizes for guessing: Krishna.

To the north of our house was a dilapidated two-storey building in which lived some Kabuli moneylenders, who were called Kabuliwallahs. Their terrace was a level below ours and every evening, I saw these tall and fierce-looking men surrender themselves before their god bending down towards the west.

Those days, many mothers would invoke the Kabuliwallah's name to control unruly children. But our neighbours were friendly towards us: an elderly Kabuli would even give us toffees, and at times, marbles and tops to me and ribbons and hairclips to my sister. He was genuinely affectionate and ever-smiling, and was a good friend of mine. However, despite the bribes, or maybe, because of them, Ruby dreaded him. Whenever she had to cross the stretch in front of the Kabuliwallahs' house, she would sprint the distance.

Occasionally, they would slaughter goats on their terrace. I watched the action with keen interest. I didn't like to watch the terrorised eyes of the goats before slaughter, but loved the spectacle of the meandering rivers of blood afterwards.

Once, when a prince from their land visited Calcutta, they invited father and me for a grand dinner. We were the only non-Kabuli guests there. The men sat opposite each other in two rows and shared food from a few large aluminium plates kept in the middle. The mutton curry was exquisite. That was the first time I had rumali rotis, which at first, I had mistaken for bundles of white cloth. Father later told me that among Muslims, the practice of the rich and the poor sharing food from the same plate was common and it was one of the reasons why the badly treated "low-caste" Hindu Bengalis had turned towards Islam.

One of the comrades of our Kabuli neighbours has been immortalised in Tagore's short story *Kabuliwallah* and later, in Tapan Sinha's film based on the story. Their fairy-tale land of chinars and the ice-cold waters of the Kabul River have been described in charming details by Syed Mujtaba Ali in a travelogue that has become a classic in Bangla: *Deshe Bideshe (At Home and Abroad)*. But the community was notorious for their usurious interest rates and strong-arm recovery tactics.

Kabuliwallahs have vanished from the life and economy of the city, replaced by equally rapacious suited executives of banks and sundry finance companies. But that dilapidated building still stands, propped up by saal trunks, as a mute witness to a pitiless banking system of the past.

There was a grocery and a workshop on the ground floor of the building. The workmen, who cleaned and repaired automobile radiators, were grimy; their singlets and trousers—they didn't wear coveralls—were smudged with grease at all times.

In the next-door grocery, the middle-aged man who sat behind a big weighing balance hung from the ceiling was an antithesis of the dirty workmen. He was always in a clean white dhoti and a starched grey shirt. He also had a dab of sandalwood paste on his forehead. It was a one-man show by the Hindi-speaking lalaji who would weigh everything from sacks of grain to handfuls of spices, put the merchandise in neat paper bags, calculate the cost faster than any cash register could, accept cash and return the balance. Whenever mother ran out of something in the kitchen, she would send me to lalaji's store. I admired his silent efficiency.

He spoke little and smiled never. Neither did I ever see him glum, unhappy, or agitated. He kept on doing the same things day after day for years. His face was impassive, almost like a mask. Running the store had possibly become automatic and natural for him, like breathing.

Almost forty years later, after we had stopped living in that house for decades, I was shocked to see him sitting behind the weighing balance with the same impassive face, wearing the same grey shirt, and sporting sandalwood paste on his forehead. Somehow, he had defied the passage of time and hadn't aged at all. Amazing!

Then the penny dropped: the man who sat before me was the son of the lalaji of yore. Incidentally, we had an almost identical anecdote in one of our Bangla textbooks. It ended with the sentence: *The tradition lives on.*

Well, it does!

10| A Plural City

In a sense, the story of Calcutta is the story of India, and the story of the so-called Third World in miniature.[vi]
– Geoffrey Moorhouse

I have written about Kabuli, Sikh, and Hindi-speaking people around us. It is a blessing to grow up in a multi-ethnic milieu because it makes one accept divergence and plurality unquestioningly.

The first census of independent India was done in the year I was born. The numbers reveal that just a third of the people in Calcutta in 1951 had been born in the city (33.2%), like me. The rest were immigrants: 12.3% from adjoining villages, 26.6% from other states, and 26.9% from East Pakistan, like my parents.[vii]

Most of the people from other states fitted themselves snugly in the economy of the city. Over at least 300 years, immigrants brought to Calcutta skill sets that were not locally available: Jewish confectioners, Chinese shoemakers and dentists, Marwari and Gujarati traders, Sikh taxi operators, cooks and plumbers from Odisha, Bihari rickshaw pullers and dairy owners, Nepali security men .... The list is long.

Among the immigrants, an important segment was a tiny group of Marwari businessmen, Bangurs, Goenkas, Mittals, and most importantly, Birlas, who, besides becoming enormously rich themselves, contributed much to building what the city of Kolkata is today. In an urban folklore we heard as children, Ghanshyam Das Birla, better known as GD Birla, the entrepreneur who had set up one of the biggest conglomerates of modern India, had come to the city with no money and a big dream. It was a true story except the "no money" bit, which was a melodramatic spin. The actual founder of the family business was Ghanshyam Das's grandfather, Shiv

Narayan Birla, who had left home and gone to Bombay with a modest capital. He was immensely successful and in 1862, he returned to build a grand mansion in his ancestral village Pilani in the Jhunjhunu district of Rajasthan. The mansion is known as Birla Haveli, an artist's impression of which you see here. It's a museum and tourist attraction today.

Therefore, Ghanshyam Das's was not a rags-to-riches story. Nevertheless, it was a story of tremendous grit and courage. He fought an unequal battle with British and Scottish jute merchants of Calcutta, who refused to cede an inch to an upstart Indian, and ultimately, got the better of them. In 1919, GD Birla became the first Indian to own a jute mill.

Later, he and his family would set up several industries around the city. The Birlas have also left their footprints across Calcutta: Birla Academy of Art and Culture, MP Birla Planetarium, and the Birla Industrial & Technological Museum. The last one my friends and I visited often when we were in high school. Entry was free.

Two immigrant communities I haven't mentioned so far were in direct competition with locally available skills. Tamil and Malayali white-collar workers competed with Bengalis and, I believe, proved themselves to be better pen-pushers than the original babus. Many intrepid young men from the South would come to the city hanging by the slender thread of an insecure, low-paying job at a private company, or simply looking for a job. Over time, by sheer grit-industry-integrity-and-intelligence, they would reach high positions in commerce and industry.

When I was old enough to go out on my own, I used to go to a park in the afternoon with my mutt, Toffee. My playmates included two boisterous Sikh boys among others. The park had a big gazebo with a sloping roof from which a few tiles had been missing. It would shelter an occasional vagabond or two. But for the gazebo and a few unpainted slides and swings, Kalighat Park had nothing that one normally associates with parks: no fountains, no flower beds, not even trimmed hedges. It was a barren tract of a brown rectangle around which ran an asphalt walkway, as prosaic as a park could be. In the space between the path and the park fencing, there were benches—wooden planks fixed on cast iron frames. There used to be hardly any elderly men in the park, and not even one elderly woman. The benches were never filled with senior citizens discussing the many ailments that they themselves and their country were suffering from. In the 1950s, not many would live long enough to enjoy leisurely strolls in the autumn of their lives. (Life expectancy at the time of our independence was around 37.) The visitors to the park were mostly boys.

A large group of older boys in their late teens came to the park every day. A beautiful teenaged girl was at the centre of the group, sending out ripples of happiness every time she smiled. Always in a long frock with floral designs, she would sit at the centre of a bench with fawning male admirers on either side, behind, and in front. A queen bee in every sense of the word, she carried herself with great poise. She had been the central character of a popular Bangla children's film *Dersho khokār kāndo (Tale of a hundred and fifty kids).*

Here is a picture from a poster for the movie. The boys had been her co-actors. She was a desert flower in that barren park.

Contrary to our expectations, she never became a film star. Half a century later in a different millennium, as I key in these lines, I wonder if she ever became an ordinary housewife who would send her children to school in the morning and freshen up in the evening and wait for her husband to return. I hope not. It would have been such a sad death of a collective dream!

Hari, my Bihari friend was an antithesis of the beautiful girl: dark, short, and stub-nosed. Hari didn't go to school; he helped his father, a fruit vendor, in his business. Once, as I was passing by, Hari was "manning" his father's basket of stock-in-trade. He gave me an orange for free.

One of my best friends Gopal was a Tamil, but spoke Bangla as naturally as any of us. He lived with his parents close to the park in a small one-room apartment over a garage. Gopal, loved by all, was a well-mannered tiny boy, who conducted himself with great dignity. Once, when a much bigger lad bullied him, he surprised everyone by challenging the bully to combat. The latter retreated, but signed off with the threat, 'Wait. I'll take care of you tomorrow.'

Gopal went home but came back within minutes. He sought out his tormentor and told him calmly, 'Let's not leave it for tomorrow. Let's settle it here and now.' So saying, the wisp of a boy rolled up his sleeves and faced his much bigger adversary.

The fight never happened; the bully was what bullies usually are: a chicken. Then Gopal told us, when his mother had heard about the quarrel, she asked him to go back and settle the matter once and for all. At that time, it did not occur to me it was an act of tremendous courage on the part of his mother. I bow to her memory.

Around Lake Market, not far from our house, lived lots of people from South India. We couldn't distinguish between Telugus, Tamils,

Malayalis, and Kannadigas. Everyone from the South was a Madrasi, which was perhaps understandable because until 1956, the Madras State included large parts of what are now four major linguistic states. The "natives" of Calcutta had a grudging respect for the Madrasis because of their discipline, hard work, low profile, and of course, amiable nature. These days in Kolkata, you rarely come across a freshly washed patch of sidewalk with an unpretentious kōlām made with rice flour in front of the main door of a South Indian home. Nobody comes to the city from Tamil Nadu or Kerala any more to make a living. The once thriving cosmopolitan city has collapsed into a cesspool of mediocrity.

Although the city of Calcutta was cosmopolitan, the Bengali middle class was arrogant and insular. Hardly anyone in my circle knew that Khotta was a dialect widely used in what was then South Bihar. But the boys in the park often referred to all Biharis by the derogatory epithet Khotta. Besides, blatantly racist names such as Uṛē for Odishis and Mēṛō for Marwaris were freely used, usually behind their backs. No less a person than Satyajit Ray used Uṛē in his film *Parashpathar (The Philosopher's Stone)*, but later, added an apology in the credits.

Incidentally, there was no Muslim boy in my class, and as far as I know, in our school. It was possibly not specific to my school. A well-known communist leader of our time, Santosh Rana has written in his autobiography[viii] that during his years in Presidency College and later in Calcutta University Science College in Raja Bazaar in the 1960s, he had no Muslim classmate.

Notwithstanding this fact and the Bengali's tendency to abuse others, sharing the city with different religions and speech communities was considered normal in my childhood. Plurality was not a subject of discussion; it was a way of life.

11| A City of Refugees, a City of Strife

Kolkata has long been a haven for uprooted people. Since its foundation during the colonial era, the city has absorbed migrants from its rural hinterland as well as through its docks. Kolkata has ... acted as a refuge not only for people: Its coffee houses and campuses have continued to nurture distinct promises of the Indian nation itself.[ix]

– James Bradbury

In the early 1940s, as Muslim League became the main political voice of Muslims in British India, the prospect of Pakistan looked increasingly real. This was the time when Hindu land-owners began migrating from the Muslim majority areas of East Bengal to Calcutta, the rest of West Bengal, and Assam. (My father might have seen the writing on the wall; he had come to Calcutta even earlier.) Since many of the new migrants had family or friends in Assam or West Bengal, it was easier for them to restart their life in these states. Some of them were able to transfer their assets, and some even bought residential properties from Bengali Muslims who had started a reverse migration towards the east around the time. Hindus left behind in East Pakistan after the Partition were largely working class and farming families, those who were on the lower levels of the social pyramid. They would keep coming over the next four decades.

In the western part of India, there was a brutal and bloody two-way exodus immediately after the Partition. While Muslims from North India moved westward, millions of Sikhs and Hindus from Sindh and West Punjab came in. The exodus there "happened in one big rush, but in Bengal, it was spread out. However, in the winter of

1949-50, there was a wave of communal violence in East Pakistan, which forced many more Hindus across the border. In previous years, 400,000 refugees came into West Bengal; in 1950, the number jumped to 1.7 million"[x].

Where did they settle down? Krishna Dutta[xi] writes:

> Then came an uncontrollable wave of refugees. … They included both the middle class and the rural poor, who had been forcibly uprooted, unlike the earlier migrants. Some—about a quarter of the 1950 influx—settled in relief camps known as "colonies". In 1949, there were more than 40 colonies in southeast Calcutta and some 65 in the north. Their "housing" consisted of temporarily built thatched huts, water drawn from a standpipe, and sanitation arrangements that were insufficient. Conditions were severely overcrowded and squalid. Yet, these shabby clusters of shelters had grand names like Adarsha Nagar (Ideal City) and Bijoy Garh (Victory Township)—the second of which still exists, though no longer as a shanty town, but as a busy southern suburb.

Several autobiographies, written by authors from historian Tapan Raychaudhuri to poet-novelist Sunil Gangopadhyay to lesser-known author Ajay Gupta, recount the struggle of the Bengali refugee. Ritwik Ghatak, who too was a refugee, captured the appalling conditions of the shanty towns of Krishna Dutta in his films.

Some of our relatives uprooted from East Bengal found new homes in a settlement way beyond the southern periphery of the city. The makeshift township, Bāghā Jatin Colony, was named after the Bengali revolutionary Jatindranath Mukherjee, who had killed a tiger (bāgh in Bangla) with just a dagger in a hand-to-paw combat and thus acquired the honorific Bāghā Jatin. Later, he was killed in Orissa in 1915 by a much stronger predator, the British police, in an unequal battle.

One evening, Aunt Anima's husband drove us to Bāghā Jatin Colony in his black Hillman Minx. After the bumpy crossing of a railway track, it was a long drive through semi-darkness along a dusty road beside which there was hardly any habitation. We stopped at a solitary roadside tea stall in the middle of an open space, which had just a kerosene lamp throwing more darkness than light.

From there on, we turned left and walked along narrow, sometimes slushy alleys in a settlement of rudimentary huts made of shaved bamboo strips with either tiles or thatch serving as roofs. There was no electricity.

That was my first visit to Ritwik Ghatak's world of the dispossessed. Let's recall that the immigrants only managed to forcibly occupy marshy lands and empty buildings, they could not occupy places in offices or factories. So, they had to eke out a meagre living by doing odd jobs, offering private tuitions, pulling cycle rickshaws, or setting up petty shops in refugee settlements where the buyer was as poor as the seller.

As they joined the ranks of job seekers, opportunities shrank for the local residents. But they bore the brunt with remarkable equanimity. They didn't target the refugee, except for occasionally hurling the pejorative moniker "Bāngāl", which roughly meant a stupid yokel. This doggerel is an innocuous if insulting mockery of the immigrants:

> The Bāngāl isn't human, it's some other creature,
> It leaps onto trees, but has no tail as a feature.

For the people in West Bengal—both old residents and immigrants—in the 1950s, the partition of India was a lot more real than her independence.

* * *

The address of the building we lived in was 139-B Russa Road, which bisected South Calcutta. Sometime in the 1950s, our address changed to 59 A, Shyama Prasad Mukherjee Road as Russa Road was divided into two and named after a father and a son: Ashutosh and Shyama Prasad Mukherjee.

Ashutosh Mukherjee, a jurist and mathematician, headed Calcutta University for 10 years in its glory days. He set up several colleges, including the University Science College. His son Shyama Prasad was a great orator and a leader of the far-right religio-political group, Hindu Mahasabha. Needless to say, he was a critic of Gandhi, Congress, and its secular politics. Yet, Jawaharlal Nehru included him in the first ministry in independent India. Shyama Prasad also set up a political party in 1951: Bharatiya Jana Sangh.

Shyama Prasad Mukherjee's death in police custody in Kashmir in 1953 shocked Calcutta. A gigantic funeral cortège—I was told—had passed by our house. However, as a child, I never heard the name of the right-wing Hindu-supremacist political party set up by Shyama Prasad, although Gandhi, Nehru, and more often, Bose were subjects of conversation. West Bengal had a sizable population of Hindus driven away from East Bengal by their Muslims neighbours, but the politics of retribution did not germinate in West Bengal.

After independence, Congress, which abandoned almost every vestige of Gandhian thoughts except for trappings like the khadi clothing, ruled continuously in Bengal until the late sixties. The political opposition in Bengal consisted of different shades of red: The Communist Party of India (CPI) and their allies like the Revolutionary Socialist Party (RSP). Between the Right and the Left, there was nobody in the centre.

The Left worked on the discontent amongst East-Bengali refugees in particular and Bengalis in general. They organised waves of meetings, processions and general strikes and turned Calcutta into a "city of processions" for the rest of India. The moniker was considered a badge of honour by many. One of my parents' senior friends, Radha Ballav Gope, whose story I am going to tell you in a moment, was a grassroot level worker of the RSP. Radha Ballav didn't know that he had sown the seeds of left politics in a little boy's mind.

From what I remember about those days, I believe politics had not entered every sphere of activity as it has now, from governing bodies of schools to sporting clubs. However, processions and meetings were part of everyday life. General strikes or hartals—the word bandh was yet to be coined—would be organised at times. On the days of general strikes, schools and offices would not function; shops would be shuttered. Public buses and trams would not ply and there would be hardly any vehicles on the eerily empty roads on which boys played football. At the crossing near our house, a bunch of young men assembled from early morning with red flags in their hands and excitement in their eyes. Their task was to stop any passing private vehicle and interrogate the passengers. If the commuters were able to establish they had serious business like a medical emergency, they would be allowed to pass unscathed. Otherwise, the tyres would be deflated. The police did not try to disperse the picketers and on the whole, the general strikes used to be pretty tame and peaceful affairs.

By day end, there would be a few immobilised cars lined up on the street. No one thought they stood as a portentous sign of an immobilised West Bengal of the future.

12| The First Rebel

Radha Ballav Gope, a political activist I met as a small child, was responsible for the first political action of my life at the age of, maybe, four.

In July 1953, when the second-class tram fares in Calcutta were increased by a paisa, the paisa used to be made of copper. Also, it was one-sixty-fourth of a rupee and not one-hundredth as it is now; the decimal system would arrive four years later, courtesy a long-term view taken by the Jawaharlal Nehru government, something that politicians aren't particularly fond of. The people of Calcutta obviously valued the paisa a great deal those days. They protested vigorously against the hike. The movement, popularly known as *Ek poisār loṛāi (the Struggle for a Paisa)*, disrupted city life completely from 1 July 1953 for about a month.[xii]

The Communist Party of India (CPI) and its allies including the Revolutionary Socialist Party (RSP) formed a committee to resist the fare hike and called a general strikes on 5 July, and then again on 15 July. What began with protesters urging commuters not to pay the higher fares and to get off trams, turned into pelting stones at tramcars and setting them on fire. The Chief Minister, Dr Bidhan Chandra Roy had to return from Vienna, where he had gone for an eye surgery, posthaste. A number of trams were burned and many died when police fired in retaliation or otherwise.

Later—I was still a small child—one day, I was on a tram with my parents. When the conductor approached us for tickets, I stood up, clenched my fist, and said, 'Bāṛti bhāṛa dicchina, debōnā!' (We won't pay the enhanced fare, never!) Mom and dad were hugely embarrassed and the people around had a hearty laugh, I was told much later. I have no recollection of the momentous event in my life.

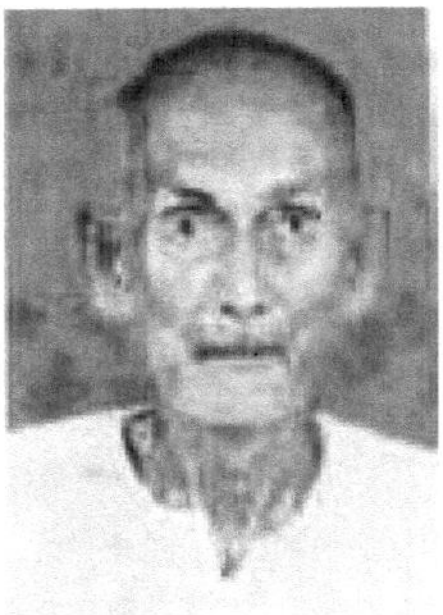

Radha Ballav Gope was one of the minor organisers of the Struggle for a Paisa. He was a thin, dark, elderly man in coarse white khadi kurta and pyjamas that were always clean but never ironed. He was possibly of medium height, but looked shorter as he had a slight stoop.

Mother called him Ballavda and he called her didi, although he was old enough to be her father. He was not related to Ma. I have no idea how their paths crossed.

Ballavda visited us regularly to distribute a weekly (or was it a fortnightly?) tabloid size newspaper. Except for the size, it had nothing in common with a tabloid. It contained eight pages of political discourse in convoluted Bangla printed in a primitive letterpress; there were no pictures. Its masthead was corrupted by thin irregular white lines—possibly an ancient wooden block was used to print it. The weekly/fortnightly was *Ganabarta (People's Voice)*, the mouthpiece of RSP. Except me, no one at home read it. I read Ganabarta ever since I got hooked to printed letters although I understood nothing in it.

Our connection with Ganabarta snapped abruptly when Ballavda passed away. In fact, I was the one who discovered Ballavda's passing when I read a four-line obituary on an inside page of a Bangla daily: *Radha Ballav Gope, a former freedom fighter who had spent many years in British jails, including the infamous Cellular Jail in the Andamans, is no more.* A pall of gloom descended on our family.

Ruby and I loved Ballavda with the kind of unconditional affection that only children are capable of offering. Whenever he came, Ma would offer him tea and snacks, which was usually a few Marie biscuits. While Ballavda talked and laughed heartily as he sipped his tea, Ruby and I gave him company. Ma treated the simple, unassuming man with great reverence, and so did Baba. When they were not around, Ruby and I could interact with him more, which we loved.

Never pressed for time, Ballavda talked at length about why poor people were poor, why one shouldn't pay the enhanced tram fares, or how unjust Lord Ram, the revered hero of the epic, had been to his wife. Ballavda treated us as human beings, not as kids. Another aspect set him apart: he laughed like a child. I have met only another adult who could laugh as innocently.

There were lots of guests in our house who stayed for a few hours to a few months. Our house had the smell of impermanence one comes across in railway waiting rooms. All our relatives and visitors treated Ballavda with some kind of special respect. Even at that tender age, I knew that people revered him not for what he had, but because he didn't have anything. Those days, money had not become the default currency for all human transactions. The spiritual cleansing that the freedom struggle had brought about was yet to evaporate completely. Mists of a vague chemical, which might be called idealism, still hung in the air. Men like Ballavda were rare even in those days, but they did exist as the fading signature of a dying time.

The last time when I saw him, Ballavda was leading a single-file procession of about fifty men on the road, protesting against something. It was one of those run-of-the-mill rallies one came across in Calcutta every other day.

Postscript: In 2009, after this story was published in *The Statesman*, Kolkata, my son discovered the following on the official website of Andaman Cellular Jail along with the photograph of Ballavda you see here.

Radha Ballav Gope Arms and Explosives Act

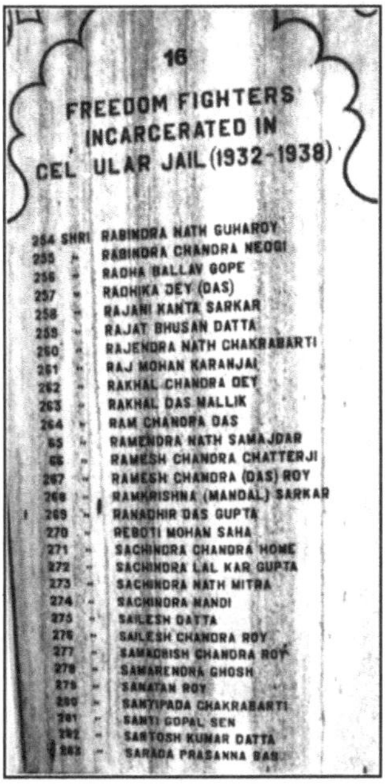

Born 1897, Domeshpur, Faridpur, Bangladesh, s/o Late Madanmohan Gope businessman. Read upto intermediate (sic). At the age of 13 joined the Anusheelan Samity. Arrested in 01.09.1933 with arms. Sentenced to 7 years prison term under Arms Act & Explosives Act. Deported to Andamans. Joined second hunger strike. Repatriated in January 1938. Participated in the hunger strike in Dum Dum Central jail in 1939 July duration 36 days. After the expiry of the sentence arrested under Defence of India rules. Released after the termination of the Second World War in 1945. Total jail period 12 years.

It is perhaps an indication of the direction India has taken of late that later, I could not find this piece of information on any government website. But this plaque in the Cellular Jail in the Andamans mentioned my mother's Ballavda. Please check the third name.

13| Music Lovers

My friends and I have been crazy about music since we were young. As we couldn't afford expensive tickets for major classical music concerts, we spent many nights listening to music sitting on newspapers spread on footpaths.[xiii]

– Sunil Gangopadhyay

Just as Nature uses the same die to create identical twins, Calcutta Telephones got all their telephone sets cast in the same die. Invariably black, they had circular dials and a heavy, dumbbell-like receiver. To become the proud owner of such a set, one had to apply for and pay a fee upfront. And then wait for an eternity before getting connected.

When we got one, it was kept in the room at the centre of our house, on a beautiful three-legged table with a circular top. The black polish of the table matched the colour of the receiver upon it. And underneath the instrument was a tapestry doily that would have made the telephone proud if it could think.

But despite the pride of place given to the instrument, there were hardly any phone calls received or made, because only a few of our relations or acquaintances had phones. Telephone owners were a rare species. And individual owners of cars were the equivalents of billionaires of the present time.

Pishemoshai, that is, my aunt Anima's husband, was one such person. He had a black Hillman Minx, a small car with a beautiful system for side-signal. On either side, in the upright between the front and rear doors, a yellow plastic bar lay sleeping. When the car turned a corner, it would jump out like a tiny arm, hang horizontally and glow. Incidentally, I knew another person who had a Hillman Minx. He was Dev Anand, one of the three superstars of Bombay. (The term Bollywood hadn't been coined.)

The more proximate Hillman, which was driven either by its handsome owner or a nattily dressed Nepali by name Samuel, was the chariot for our rare forays to the other half of the world, that is, to events like ice skating or a game of polo. For many years, aunt worked in London and made trips to India every two years or so. Once, Ruby and I accompanied Pishemoshai to the airport to see off aunt when she was returning to London. On our way back, Pishemoshai took us to the Trincas, an upmarket restaurant in Park Street, where the budding singer Usha Iyer (Uthup) would mesmerise young men some years later. It was shortly before noon on a Sunday; the place was almost empty. A European couple were dancing on the wooden floor to the beat of recorded music. (The music was possibly from a jukebox.) The city of Calcutta hadn't yet become an international pariah. It had a significant population of Anglo-Indians who were considered sahibs by most "natives". European tourists were often seen on the streets of the city.

In the Trincas, Ruby and I ate banana split: half a banana cut along its length and stashed between two slabs of ice cream generously sprinkled with crunchy nuts. For a long time, I couldn't get over the surprise of discovering a banana in an ice cream! During the entire childhood, it was our only foray into an air-conditioned restaurant with waiters in fancy livery.

Unlike the telephone or the car, the gramophone, seen in many homes, was a defining symbol of middle-class happiness. The sole manufacturers of the device, *His Master's Voice, HMV* in short, coined a slogan that became a Bangla catchphrase: *Sukhī grihōkōn, shōbhē gramophone.* Literally translated, it reads: *Happiness is shown, when there's a gramophone!*

Happiness became visible in our house shortly after an attempt by dad to buy a radio, a story I'll tell you soon. The heavy gramophone was housed in a beautifully polished brown wooden cabinet in which a spiralling speaker was hidden behind a golden wire mesh. Like most fancy stuff in our home (except the telephone), it had been bought second-hand. The timbre was magnificent.

Technology moved slowly during my childhood, like time itself. The gramophone in our home was not very different from the first "talking machine" with spiral grooves on a flat rotating disc, invented by German-American Emile Berliner in 1887. Incidentally, it was Berliner who named the instrument gram-o-phone or gramophone. Our turntable was identical to the one writer Ruskin Bond had used as a child two decades before.

> We had a beautiful gramophone .... It was one of those wind-up affairs, and you had to change the needle from time to time. The turntable took only one 78 rpm record, so you just couldn't relax and listen to an uninterrupted programme of music. You were kept busy all the time—changing records, changing needles and constantly winding the machine vigorously so that it wouldn't fade away in the middle of a song.[xiv]

A younger cousin of my father gifted us a record of Pandit Dattatreya Vishnu Paluskar, which had the bhajans *Chalo man, Ganga-Yamuna teer* and *Thumaka Chalata Ramachandra* on two sides.

It was bigger than the usual 78 RPM record. Occasionally, uncle would visit us and listen to the songs with a wistful look in his eyes. He obviously couldn't afford a gramophone at home. Tamal Kaku—I would learn later—had been a talented singer who could not pursue a musical career as he had to take care of several siblings at a young age, besides resettling in an unknown city.

One of them, Rakhal, did take music seriously. He was a disciple of Pandit Bhimsen Joshi. Whenever we went to their home in Bhawanipur, we found him doing riyaaz alone on a bare cot, with the accompaniment of a tanpura, sweating profusely in a darkish room that had neither a window, nor a fan. A set of tablas used to lie around. I didn't care much for the music, but often sat transfixed watching a man immersed in his passion. One day, I decided to slam the tabla randomly to make the music more interesting. The singer screwed up his face in disgust and asked me to get lost.

Rakhal Kaku did not become a well-known singer because he died in his thirties, possibly because of substance abuse.

* * *

In the 1950s and 60s, classical music concerts were often held in Calcutta theatres. In the winter, they were organised in make-shift open-air auditoriums. One of my numerous uncles—possibly the music lover Tamal Kaku's younger brother Kajal—once took me to a programme of classical music. We all sat cross-legged on hessian mats covered with milk-white sheets in a large pandal. Every inch of that large make-shift auditorium was taken up by eager listeners who sat with rapt attention in pin-drop silence. There were lots of people outside the concert too. Amplifiers were provided so that people outside could enjoy the music for free as they braved the nippy Calcutta winter under an open sky while dew dropped.

I fell asleep as soon as the first singer began his slow, relaxed prelude … and was woken up when the concert ended and darkness was giving way to light. Sunil Gangopadhyay, the much-loved Bengali novelist and poet whose lines I have used above, was 17 years older than me. Did he sit awake through the night listening to classical music sitting on a newspaper spread on the footpath while I slept inside?

Although I heard nothing that night, the seriousness of the audience was permanently etched in my mind. Much later, when I went to hear the Pakistani singer Mehdi Hassan at an indoor stadium in Hyderabad, I was shocked to see vendors selling tea and peanuts and people talking even while Hassan was offering his mellifluous gazals. It would have been unthinkable in Calcutta. Incidentally, Sunil Gangopadhyay wrote:

> Before Ravi Shankar and Ali Akbar, there were not many Bengali musicians in the Indian classical music scene, but Bengalis were known as discerning music lovers. Much later, I heard from Ustad Amir Khan that in his time, unless a musician was received warmly by the Bengali audience, he or she would find it difficult to find their feet at the national level.[xv]

The musical world of the city had space for the less highbrow genres too. On Sundays, Pankaj Kumar Mallick conducted a programme on the All India Radio (AIR) to train budding musicians. People listened to the programme with utmost seriousness, although most of them didn't fancy their chances of becoming singers. Mother was one of them.

The AIR was the only entity of its kind. It had an impact that is impossible to imagine in an era of countless TV/radio stations dishing out mostly mediocre stuff. The AIR was snooty too. They shunned film songs until they were forced to start *Vividh Bharati*, which arrived in 1957 to combat Radio Ceylon. Radio Ceylon had filled the vacuum by recording programmes of film songs like *Binaca Geetmala* in a Bombay studio. However, unlike the present-day RJs, the presenters then hardly tried to build a rapport with their audience. Ameen Sayani, the presenter of *Binaca Geetmala*, was an honourable exception.

Surprisingly, despite having no competition in other Indian languages, the AIR didn't drift into lazy complacency. The high standards of their productions were apparent even to us children.

The Durga Puja celebrations began on *the Mahalaya*, that is, the first day of the lunar month in which the Puja is held. That morning, almost the entire Bangla-speaking people of the country would wake up in the small hours to listen to a musical programme presented by the Calcutta station of the AIR. Every year, without fail. Do you know of another radio programme that has alone enthralled millions year after year?

In the morning of the Bengali New Year, a music programme was held in the theatre opposite our house, Basusree. Almost all the famous popular singers and film stars participated in the concert, and there too, they had just a guy announcing the name of the next artiste in a dull monotone. It would begin with junior artistes and as it went on, more formidable singers like Sandhya Mukherjee and Shyamal Mitra would take the stage. The last slot was always reserved for Hemanta Mukherjee. Adoringly called Hemanta in Bengal and Hemant Kumar in the rest of India, he looked like a middle-aged academic in a white dhoti and long shirt and oversized glasses in heavy black frames. His baritone was magical.

The theatre seated around five hundred people and at least ten times as many gathered outside. Like in the classical music programmes, funnel-shaped loudspeakers were fitted outside. The crowd ignored the scorching April sun and stood on the pavement for hours to soak in the pleasure of live music, and to catch a glimpse of film actors in flesh and blood. A ripple of excitement swept through them whenever a star turned up. The greatest excitement and the loudest applause were always reserved for Hemanta Mukherjee and Uttam Kumar.

14| Life Lessons

People make mistakes in life through believing too much,
but they have a damned dull time if they believe too little.[xvi]
– James Hilton

As I write this memoir, it's time to acknowledge my debt to the people who taught me in classrooms and outside to make me what I am. You would have come across some of them already. Let me now try to recall their special qualities which made deep impressions on me. And introduce you to a few more.

My ordinary middle-class parents, besides teaching me to live simply and not to be greedy, helped me fall in love with reading, which perhaps was their greatest gift.

My early-childhood nanny Sudhadi and her husband Rajenda made an indelible impression on me. A person with deep compassion, Sudhadi might have rubbed off some of it on to me. And as I have said, Rajenda was a fascinating man who had had an accident that turned him from a highly skilled worker into an odd-jobs man. But he didn't wallow in self-pity. Rather, he enjoyed every moment of his much-diminished life. Thank you Rajenda for teaching me not to complain, to take the rough with the smooth.

Another multipurpose employee in my dad's small business was Motilal, a thin man of indeterminate age with a toothless smile. He taught me an adage much before I read it: *Never take life too seriously; you won't come out of it alive.* Motilalda rarely spoke the truth, but I believe he lied just for the fun of telling a good tale. From him I learned there is always an imaginary world right after the next turn in the road. That world might not be as exotic as James Hilton's *Shangri La*, but Shangri La existed all the same. In short, he taught me the basic truth that imagination is another element of reality.

Don't mathematicians too need an imaginary number to go with the real one?

Although freedom fighter Ballavda was a communist, looking back, I see a glimpse of Gandhi in the simple khadi-clad elderly man who had no personal possession and possibly lived in a commune of political workers. As a child, at some point in my mind, his bald pate, round glasses, and innocent smile got merged with Gandhiji's autographed toothless photo that hung in my father's study. Radha Ballav's minimalist life dedicated to others made a deep impression in the child that I was.

In the primary section of Ballygunge Government High School, every teacher was excellent. I do not recall their names or most other details, but if I close my eyes, even now I can see our headmistress, Aparna Dasgupta, an exceedingly beautiful woman with curly black hair. Aparnadi commanded awe and respect without the least effort. Early in my life, she imparted an invaluable leadership lesson to me: Quietness too could be a tool in the hands of a strong leader.

School buses hadn't become mandatorily yellow yet. In my first school, Victoria Institution, the buses were green. In the only other school I studied at, they were dark blue. Hiralal Babu was the driver of one such blue school bus I took from Class III to V. To avoid distraction likely to be caused by the racket a bunch of kids might produce, Hiralal babu wouldn't allow us to open our mouths while we were on the bus. The discipline was imposed in an extremely rude manner by the driver and his assistant; it was my first brush with tyranny.

Ever since, I have hated tyranny of all kinds.

* * *

I was fortunate to be born in a family that had several strong and professionally successful women. Given the kind of influence they had on me as a child, I was destined to be a respecter of women, if not a gynolator.

The first name that comes to my mind is Suprabha Chaudhuri, mother's only aunt. She was the principal of one of the oldest women's colleges in Calcutta for as long as I can remember. Literature was her bread and butter, but she was, I think, a great administrator too. She ran a huge college seemingly with ease. At the same time, she was most affectionate towards her niece and her children. As a child, one couldn't have had a better role model.

Aunt Jana is from what is now the Czech Republic. An epitome of hard work, she has an exceptionally sensible, no-nonsense head on her shoulders. When I met her, I got to learn how the mind of a child of an industrialised country might work. Like everybody else in her husband's family, her husband, my uncle Apu too was a Luddite. He would think twice even before changing the lens of an SLR camera. His wife on the contrary was completely fearless about technology; she would repair everything from a broken umbrella to a radio. Later, once when my mother was alone in their London home during a severe winter, the central heating of their stand-alone house failed. Mother knew there wasn't much point in calling her bro. So, she called Jana at her office. Jana asked her guest to prepare a mug of black coffee and drove home. She had the coffee, climbed up to the central heating unit, and fixed it.

Once Jana said that during a holiday, the hotel they stayed in didn't provide a coffee maker in room. So she joined a few hairpins to improvise a water heater. She added, 'Of course, a student of physics won't approve of it.' I didn't tell her that most of the physics we studied was printed letters. It had little room for water heaters or anything else of practical significance.

Nearer home, a rock-solid feminine figure was Smriti Pishi, Dr Mamata Chaudhuri, my father's younger cousin who happened to be a childhood friend of my mom in Karimgunj, a small town in Sylhet. If you look at the present map of India, you will find Kolkata and Karimgunj on opposite sides across Bangladesh. Smriti Pishi's father was a school teacher who thought it fit to send his oldest daughter to study medicine in faraway Calcutta in the 1940s. Daughter didn't fail him. She graduated, became a successful physician, married a brilliant colleague, and inspired her younger siblings. Rare would be a family in all of Bengal those days that produced three doctors and three graduate engineers among nine offspring.

Dr Chaudhuri was trained in paediatrics in the USA. As a child, I saw her driving her black Ford Prefect to hospital, where she also taught paediatrics. My sister and I were under her care as infants and so would be my children. It was then that I would come to know that Smriti Pishi was a strong votary of breast feeding; she detested commercial baby food. A schoolmaster's daughter from a small town, the reality of the indigent India was still at her heart. She would always tell my wife about the sources of nutrition for infants from everyday food that was better than commercial products.

Her cousin, my dad's sister Anima too was exceptional. A natural leader, Anima rose from humble beginnings to become a successful business professional, a rare specimen among the women of her generation. She and her husband, a businessman (of the Hillman Minx fame!), were the only well-off close relations we had. Both were generous. Those days, many of our relatives and acquaintances uprooted from East Bengal were trying to rebuild their lives in difficult circumstances. For many of them, Aunt Anima was a bulwark; she contributed in a big way for many a wedding in the family and outside. (Strangely, the other problem that people find challenging today, that is, healthcare, was a lot more affordable then as government hospitals were free and easily accessible; healthcare hadn't become a pitiless profit-driven industry.) Towards the end, aunt went through a bad financial patch. During one of those days, once when she was in a ruminating mood, she told me, 'I was just counting the number of gold necklaces I gave as wedding gifts. I could recall up to 15.'

Another remarkable quality she had in abundance was self-confidence. Once, a child of one of her colleagues went missing. When police couldn't find the little boy even after three days, aunt dodged past several layers of security and literally barged into the Chief Minister's room in the state secretariat. The CM then, Mr Jyoti Basu was not just another chief minister. A formidable figure, his name inspired awe. Aunt told him bluntly, 'Sir, what kind of a police force are you heading? How can they not find a lost child in the state capital in three days?'

The boy was to be found soon, loitering in a park far away from his home..

Here's another anecdote about my aunt's supreme self-assurance. My office was in downtown Calcutta then. One day, she asked me to wait for her after office as she wanted to buy curtain cloth for her home; she wanted me to help her decide. When I got into her car, she said, 'Let's drop shopping today. I have only ₹10 in my purse.'

We are talking about a time long before credit/debit cards came to India. After a few minutes, she changed her mind and asked the driver to take a U-turn. One of the biggest stores selling furnishing those days was in Little Russel Street. In the transaction that was to follow, aunt put herself in a pole position by declaring she would require 70 metres of the same cloth. Would the store be able to offer enough choice for that kind of volume? Or would she go to the wholesale market?

'No problem madam, we have lots of varieties.'

In the hour that followed, a small hillock rose on the trading counter as aunt made shop assistants show everything that she thought could be considered. Finally, she made up her mind and asked the salesman to cut the cloth.

Till then I had been standing by passively, giving my opinion when demanded. But at that point, I started feeling jumpy. Had she forgotten she had nothing in her purse? But Aunt went on, undaunted. Her decision was final, 'Yes, I said 70 metres. Okay, make it 75.'

A pair of scissors was inches away from the cloth and my heart was in my throat when aunt said, 'Just a moment!'

As the shop assistant raised his brow, she stopped for a long moment and said, 'Rather, snip off a corner and give it to me as a sample. Let me show it to my husband. He will of course accept what I select, but if I bought the whole lot and took it home, he could raise hell.'

15| A Radio, Two Confused Kids, and Their Dad

Children begin by loving their parents; as they grow older, they judge them; sometimes they forgive them.[xvii]
– Oscar Wilde

When my dad's sister Anima returned home after working in London for some years, she brought along some gadgets that boggled our collective mind.

You might recall that Aunt gave me a to-scale steel replica of a London double-decker. To mom, she gave a (Prestige) pressure cooker, something the delighted recipient hadn't heard of. On its black Bakelite handle, the time required for cooking different foodstuff was printed in white: meat—15 minutes, potatoes—3 minutes, etc. Aunt also brought a Grundig tape recorder with two large spools. One summer evening in her flat, Aunt, her husband, and Dad struggled and sweated profusely to record something on the machine. They had no clue how to go about it. Many suggestions were offered, tried, and rejected. Suddenly, the machine started replaying the animated conversation on how to run it. I think I also heard a chuckle in the background. Could it be a sneaking preview of the twenty-first century, when electronic gadgets would routinely mock people, particularly the elderly for their stupidity?

On another day, Ma's childhood friend Bela-Mashi—who visited us often—took out from her handbag a small rectangular object. What looked like a fancy tiffin box in a leather case completely

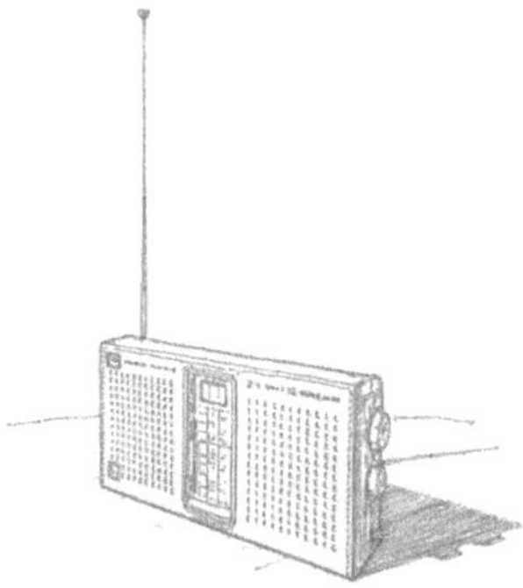

wowed us for two reasons. First, the small object was a radio! Second, it required neither a power source, nor an aerial. Yet another future shock imported by someone who had visited Japan.

The story I am going to tell you now happened even before the transistor radio arrived; when the now-omnipresent TV or mobile phone was an unimaginable future. The mobile phone, particularly the smartphone, has been the science fiction writers' collective Waterloo. While the submarine or space travel was quite accurately predicted by sci-fi writers from Jules Verne to Arthur C. Clarke, even the fertile brains of hundreds of them failed to imagine a handheld device that could not only record movies but transmit them in real time!

Back in the time I am writing about, housewives turned on their usually massive GEC, Phillips, or Murphy radio sets in the afternoon to listen to plays broadcast by the All India Radio while enjoying their well-deserved siesta. A baby's face seen in Murphy adverts, popularly known as the Murphy Baby, was possibly the most familiar face in India after Gandhi's! Atop many roofs, you would see a narrow wire mesh hanging between two high poles. These were aerials through which pre-transistor radio receivers accessed signals. They were a pain in the neck for kite flyers, but I had no problem. There was no aerial on our roof.

Mother, who sometimes gave radio talks, often saw a radio in her dreams. She passed it on to her children. A radio became—in today's parlance—a "felt need" in the family. But in the absence of an ingredient, the need hadn't turned into what economists call "demand". So, there was much excitement on the day Baba announced he was going to buy a radio.

One afternoon, sister and I accompanied dad on mission *Bring*

Home a Radio. Our destination was a store off the Central Avenue.

The jazzy showroom had arrays of radios, gramophones, and radiograms. Neither Ruby nor I had been to such a store earlier; we made the most of the good time by sinking ourselves into a plush sofa while Baba went around and discussed with a shop assistant the merits of different sets. At length, he selected a radio and called us to see and hear it. It was a fairly large Phillips, or may be, GEC receiver. Like most good radios those days, this one was housed in a wooden cabinet; the timbre was rich. It looked good too, with a big elliptical speaker showing through the silkscreen in front and piano-key switches that were the latest at the time. We were thrilled at the prospect of having such a heavenly device in our home, where till then, the only electrical appliances were incandescent bulbs much like what Edison had invented, noisy DC ceiling fans, and an electric stove with a naked coil that looked red and angry when turned on.

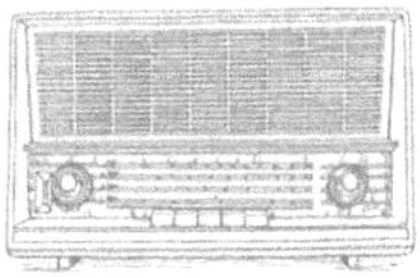

Before paying cash, Baba asked the store assistant to put it on hold for a minute. We thought he was weighing the option of buying another set. He asked us to wait and went out. Through the glass front of the showroom, we could see Baba pacing back and forth on the footpath, smoking a cigarette. The afternoon turned into evening. He lit another cigarette. He went on and on.

After a millennium, he came back, said something to the store assistant, and turned towards us. We were expecting to take a taxi. But dad returned home by bus without a radio and with two thoroughly dejected children. The missed cab ride added a minor insult to a massive injury!

To make things even worse, the next day, Dad bought a small second-hand radio set with a cracked dial. He might have picked it up from a junk dealer. We could hear mostly static through it.

I hated Baba then for ditching us at the last moment. I was too young to understand why he did what he did.

***

Old proverbs are tiny urns carrying gigantic truths. For example, consider this:

> There are three stages in a man's life. As a young boy, he believes, 'My dad knows everything.' Then comes a time when he says, 'My dad? He knows nothing!' But inevitably at some point he starts telling you, 'My father used to say ….'

Long after my father's passing, I began thinking of him often … and of the bitter-sweet relationship we shared. Salvador Dali famously said, "I won't die completely when I die." Although ordinary people do not leave behind a time-defying oeuvre of paintings, they too do not die completely when they die. For example, my father lives in my memory, and in the minds of a few others. Baba, who always wore khadi, rolled his own cigarettes, and smoked with a religious fervour, didn't do anything extraordinary in life that would justify telling his story to the world. Yet, given the odds, the mere fact that he survived with dignity was extraordinary.

He had a tough childhood after losing his old man at the age of 11. Then onward, as I've written, he and his mother struggled to make ends meet. After graduating from school, Baba had the foresight to move to Calcutta for higher studies, although he had little idea how his studies would be funded. While still a student, he did everything possible to eke out a living: from managing boarding houses to making rubber-stamps to drafting legal documents for businessmen. (Strangely, he never offered "private tuitions", the road most travelled by struggling educated young men in our part of the world.) During his many years of living in grinding poverty, he acquired a mortal fear of spending a large sum of money in one go. Consequently, he acquired no assets in his lifetime.

His boat continued to sail on choppy waters after the Second World War and the Partition of India. As he fought a grim battle all his life, he had his moments of success, but suffered more failures; several of his off-beat business ventures died in the vine.

But every evening after supper, he would put his problems aside, retire to his study, and read until early morning. The desk he sat at during the day turned into a bed without mattress, where he would lie prone with an air pillow under his chest and a book in front in an unusual bookstand. (It might well have been designed by him; I haven't seen another similar bookstand physically or through Google search.) He used to read everything that came between two covers. For example, for a brief period, he got seriously interested in palaeobotany. Generally, he was interested in spiritualism and English grammar and usage. For some reason, he never touched fiction. Long ago when I didn't know it, he managed to kindle an interest in the English language in my mind. But at times, I wish that instead, he had kindled in me an interest in making money!

Deeply interested in poetry, he often recited poems in the two languages he knew, and Sanskrit slokas.. The book I saw him reading most often was Palgrave's *Golden Treasury*, besides an eight-volume leather-bound encyclopaedia, *The Book of Knowledge*, and the *Encyclopedia Americana.* Many a time I heard Baba recite these Thomas Gray lines:

> Full many a gem of purest ray serene
> The dark unfathom'd caves of ocean bear:
> Full many a flower is born to blush unseen,
> And waste its sweetness on the desert air.

Did Father know that he too was an unsung hero?

16| Food, (No) Wine, and Guests

These recollections are from a time when middle-class Indian families couldn't imagine some of the luxuries that are taken for granted today. A pressure cooker or a transistor radio didn't exist; an air-conditioner didn't exist even in middle-class dreams. Our family and many others like ours spent most of their earnings on food. Most homes had no refrigerators; food was cooked twice a day by housewives or domestic helps. Domestic helps were economically more viable than a fridge.

Bengalis ate rice, dal, and vegetables at lunch and supper. Fish, being relatively inexpensive, was a part of our meals. For many years, I used to look forward to Sunday mornings, when I would take ₹4 from Ma and stand in a queue to buy a kilogram of mutton. As there were no pressure cooker, meat would be boiled over an hour in a wok; consequently, if you walked through the city in a Sunday morning, you would often be greeted by a tempting umami smell.

Chicken was a rare delicacy and used to cost a lot more, possibly twice as much as mutton. Eggs too were relatively pricey. At our home, eggs would be hard boiled and then deftly cut into two along the length using a thread. Half an egg was the norm.

Milk was a minor existential challenge faced by every family. As milkmen with cows or buffalos were driven out of town gradually around the year 1960, a government-run dairy farm 50 kilometres away from Calcutta became the sole supplier of milk to the metropolis. Early morning, trucks loaded with clanging glass milk bottles in steel shelves would reach the city, fan out to every corner of it, and start unloading them at milk booths, which were green wooden shacks built on footpaths. For their daily quota of milk, families had to procure a "card" after overcoming almost insurmountable obstacles, including meeting ministers at times.

Queues were as much a part of the common man's life as mobile phones are today. Early in the morning, long queues would form before milk booths, where people would return the previous day's empty bottles in exchange for that day's quota. Often, some bottles would break as the truck moved on bumpy roads, leaving behind narrow white rivers on roads. Those who reached late would return without milk. Hence, the day in Calcutta began with a mad rush to be ahead in the queue before the milk booth. A painful way to begin, particularly in winters. Then there were weekly queues in front of ration shops for rice, cooking oil, sugar, and kerosene.

In the morning, (usually) a male member of the family would go to the local bazaar, where there were no queues, just a bit of jostling. Vegetables and fruits were easily available. Bananas were found through the year, and mangoes, guavas, and oranges during seasons. Apples, pears, and grapes, though available, used to cost a bomb; they were expected to be eaten only when you were unlikely to live much longer. I distinctly remember having bought one apple when I was in high school. It cost fifty paise. Dry fruits, except raisins, were an unimaginable luxury. if memory isn't playing me false, I didn't see almonds, walnuts, and pistachios in my childhood.

In the early 21st century when I am writing this, almost all these and more are available in abundance; even the poor can afford milk and eggs, and to a lesser extent, poultry and fruits. This fantastic achievement of independent India, despite the population having increased three-fold, usually goes unnoticed.

* * *

In my childhood, if people wished to visit a friend or relative's home, there was no question of giving prior intimation as no one had telephone at home. If unfortunately the target hosts weren't at home, the visitors would uncomplainingly go to someone else's house. As we lived on a main road at the centre of the city, we had guests almost every evening. And I don't recall anyone being unhappy about it.

Mother had a band of loyal friends who would often visit us. Except Bela Mashi (who wowed us with a transistor radio), others were much younger than Ma. They too were school teachers, who Ma had met while doing different professional courses. They would spend hours together in infinite bliss and their friendship remained till death did them part. Looking back, I think the warmth of esprit de corps was more abundant then. The social media of today is a poor substitute.

We also had a few stay-in guests in our home not infrequently. For supper, the family, except for grandma, sat on heavy wooden chairs around a stout dining table. Dad had picked them up cheap from some auction house. Dining tables were uncommon in Bengali households those days. Most families would eat from bell metal plates sitting on the floor on small rugs or wooden planks. For us, bell metal plates gave away to porcelain pretty early. It might not be irrelevant to write here that I do not recall an evening when there were only four of us for an evening meal. More often than not, there would be a guest or two. And this I believe was the situation in many middle-class families. Guests were welcome. On sunny days, on rainy days. I recall, the Bengali writer Sunil Gangopadhyay wrote, his family would sit down for supper with an extra plate on the table. If a guest arrived unexpectedly, he would point at the empty plate and say, 'Ah! We were waiting for you. Do sit down.'

The generosity of people went beyond casual meals. Many successful Bengalis managed to have decent education in one of the two centres of learning in Bengal, Dhaka or Calcutta, only because they were provided with free board and lodging by distant relatives or just neighbours who had made it big in the city. The benefactors would usually provide the bare necessities to the non-paying guests, but that was enough. This system of informal scholarships was an important strength of an economy bled white by colonialism, and later, during the devastation brought about by the sudden and arbitrary partition of the country.

Let me close this chapter with an anecdote. One evening, when my dad's sister happened to be with us, there were five of us at the dining table. I remember the time too, because I heard my aunt narrate the story on several occasions. It was 10 PM and Aunt said to my dad, 'Dada, this is an unusual day for us. There is no guest at our dinner.'

As she spoke, the calling bell rang.

17| Wheels of Unchange

The hand-pulled rickshaw has become extinct, except in Kolkata and New York, as far as I have seen. But in the Big Apple, they are not a serious mode of transport; they are just a mechanism to fleece tourists, just as cycle rickshaws are in Paris. However, in Kolkata, manual rickshaws, although their number has declined, are an accepted mode of transport even now, a definitive symbol of a city living in the past. However, these days, lots of people shun the hand-pulled rickshaw as it is considered politically incorrect.

Fifty years ago, people were okay with the idea of a man pulling another. In the morning, men were often seen carrying two bags overflowing with vegetables travelling by rickshaws from the bazaar to their homes. In narrow alleys where no buses went, rickshaws were the only mode of public transport. I think they were cheap and the pullers earned a pittance for all the hard work they did. But they extracted their pound of flesh when the city went under water after heavy showers, which happened often between July and September.

Many rickshaw pullers—most of them from Bihar—slept on the footboards of their rickshaws, curled up like well-cooked shrimps. For their main meals, they ate a dough of powdered Bengal gram with salt and chillies. At quiet street corners, you would often find a man sitting with a weighing scale, a few shining aluminium plates, salt, chillies, a bagful of powdered gram, and an earthen pot of drinking water. Rickshaw pullers and other manual labourers used to have their meals there. Those were possibly the most basic eateries in the history of humankind.

The black-and-yellow taxis of my childhood were mostly Land Masters and later, Ambassadors, but there were a few large Dodges and Buicks too. The latter were the "big taxis", which were costlier.

They would easily take in seven passengers. Taxis of my childhood ran strictly by the meter and were often driven by amiable elderly Sardars, who had impeccable manners. A lone woman would board a taxi driven by a Sardarji without apprehension. The elderly drivers' white beards fluttered like flags of eternal peace. One afternoon, when I was crossing the road in front of our house recklessly, a Sardar taxi driver had to brake suddenly to save my life. Strangely, he smiled at me. I was too nervous to hear what he said to me, but a deep blue turban and a smiling face got etched in my memory. Sardar taxi drivers of Calcutta have been replaced by men from Bihar and eastern Uttar Pradesh, depriving the city of one of its most charming faces of responsible citizenry.

Most trams had two cars, the "first class" in front and the "second class" behind, which was cheaper and had no cushions on wooden seats. The communist government that ruled West Bengal continuously for over three decades from 1977 could have made trams a classless society, but didn't. Long ago I read a report in *the Statesman* that Calcutta Tramways Company (CTC) was recognised by an international body as one of the finest transport systems in the world. The tramcars, which were spanking clean, had large windows the shutters of which were hidden in a slot below. They were packed in the peak hours, but in other times, you would often find a seat. Despite being airy and light, trams had ceiling fans in wire-mesh cages in the first class. Above the windows, there were panels with neat, hand-painted adverts. Conductors were in smart khaki uniform. From outside, the shape and colour of the lights above the driver's cabin would tell you which depot the tram was headed to. Square red light to Tollygunge, and so on. A friend, Damodar, who lived in Calcutta as a child, reminds me that when a tram was blocked by another vehicle, the driver would use a tinkling bell, which was (and still is) quite unique. "Unlike airhorns," my friend writes, "the bell was pleasant, polite, and unobtrusive, as if it was saying, 'Excuse me, could you please move a bit and let me have my rails? You have the privilege of the entire carriageway, but I have only the rails. Thank you!'"

The first tramcar rolled out at four in the morning and by the time the last one returned to the depot, the city was fast asleep. They continued to be punctual until the seventies, when one of my friends, Jyoti, who worked at a jute mill outside the city, would take the first tram at Park Circus at four in the morning towards the Sealdah railway station. In the four years he worked for the mill, CTC let him down only once in a morning of torrential rain.

The Kalighat tram depot was a little farther down the road from our house, on the same side of the road. Once, late in the night, there was a big commotion when a sleepy tram driver turned his tramcar into the petrol station next to our house, thinking he had reached his destination.

The only other public transport were buses. There were private buses when I was very small, but over time, they were replaced by "state buses" everywhere in the city. The buses too were well maintained and clean. They were always red and sported the CSTC (Calcutta State Transport Corporation) logo with the head of a Royal Bengal Tiger near the entrances. Many of them were imported British Leyland double-deckers, on one of which my journey for this memoir began.

The Chief Minister of West Bengal then, Dr Bidhan Chandra Roy was unlike Bengalis. He spouted no philosophy, but did solid work like setting up industries, residential townships, a major dairy farm, and engineering colleges, including the first IIT in Kharagpur (in a former prison housing freedom fighters) and Jadavpur University. Under Dr Roy, there was a spurt of industrialisation in West Bengal, the principal among which was Durgapur Steel Plant.

Ambassador taxis, about which I have just written, (and cars) were manufactured at the Hindustan Motors factory near Calcutta set up by Braj Mohan Birla, a brother of the legendary Ghanshyam Das, in 1948. The Ambassador, a large sedan which was a version of the Morris Oxford, was a technologically advanced vehicle in the 1950s. Later, in the Nehruvian "licence-permit-raj" environment where no new competitor could come up, the company never felt the need for a technology upgrade for their cars (or their Bedford trucks and buses). It got consigned to history in no time when the Indian economy opened up in the 1990s and a number of international car makers set up production lines in India. While the hand-pulled rickshaw represents stagnation, the shell of the once thriving car factory and a railway station named Hind Motor now stand as a forlorn sign of the industrial decline of West Bengal.

As a child, I neither knew nor cared for the other initiatives of Dr Bidhan Chandra Roy, but CSTC was a part of my everyday world. Dr Roy had set up the transport company and employed refugees from East Pakistan to run the buses. They were also known as *Bidhan Babur bus.*

I travelled by a *Bidhan Babur bus* every day for a year.

18| Challenges in a Boys' School

As I have written, the beginning of my schooling was simply splendid. With 30 girls in my class, I was the only boy. And among my lovely classmates, I had an almost serious relationship with a beautiful dark girl called Leena.

Victoria Institution, a school and college for girls, was named after the Queen of England who ruled India from 1876 to 1901. They admitted boys up to Class IV. As my mother taught there, I was enrolled there in Class II. After I left the school a year later, Leena used to enquire about me from mom as long as she (Leena) was in the school. Could I be so fortunate that she would read this?

The *tin nombor bus,* i.e., the Bus No. 3 that mom and I took every morning passed by an open space where a big building was being constructed. There, a monster crane used to ram down long vertical steel joists into the ground every minute or so. The hammer, which would be dropped through a casing from a great height, would fall on the head of a joist with a bang. I would eagerly wait to see the spectacle of the hammer falling as the bus passed by. On days I couldn't see it, I would feel dejected. At that time, I couldn't have known that someday, a new chapter of my life would begin at the building which would come up upon those joists; that much later, I would attend a job interview on the thirteenth floor of the first Calcutta high-rise, *Jeevandeep* in Chowringhee Road.

I took admission tests for Class III at two boys' schools near home, one of which was St. Lawrence High School. There, the first question was "Write down your name." I wrote. The second task was to write my father's name. After writing the first two letters, I stopped because I didn't know how to write the compound Bengali consonant that was a part of Baba's name. I believed I wasn't allowed to answer the third question without answering the second, so I didn't bother to read the remaining questions … I doodled until the test ended. It was the first recorded failure in my life.

When I joined Ballygunge Government High School, Dad fudged my date of birth. Consequently, in official records, I am a year younger than what I am. As far as I know, it was the only instance when my old man did something dishonest. And he did it with an eye on my future. Those days, a government or quasi-government job was considered the only means of survival for a middle-class halfwit like me. To achieve the moksha, one had to be 24 years or younger. For every job on offer at the end of a complex, year-long obstacle race, there were tens of thousands of contenders. Therefore, reducing the age of an offspring by a year meant they would get an extra (undeserving) opportunity to grab the pot of gold. The practice was not unusual. In fact, I knew a gentleman (Bless his soul!) who retired seven years after his mother did! Since I love to blow my own trumpet, let me add that dad's apprehension was needless. I managed to secure a decent job in my first, rather perfunctory attempt.

Most of my classmates in Ballygunge Government High School came from families of teachers, doctors, and government or private sector employees. Our teachers too were archetypal middle-class Bengali intellectuals, mostly dressed in everyday dhoti and kurta or shirt. They came to school by public bus. But the school hadn't been like that always. Historian and Oxford don, Tapan Raychaudhuri studied there about 25 years before, in pre-independence India. In his autobiography Raychaudhuri wrote:

> Quite a few among the teachers came 'suited and booted', as we say in Anglo-Bengali. Those who came in Indian attire certainly did not wash their dhoti and kurta in soda ash, nor use their pillows as substitute for ironing. The place was posh, to put it briefly. ... Some of the students came in big cars and spoke fluent English. Their noses were most certainly in the air. ... A few belonged to the families of rajas and maharajas.[xviii]

When I was in the school, no one came in big cars and barring exceptions, nobody was stuck-up. Therefore, I got the opportunity to soak in the delightful potion called "middle-class values" for nine years. But as a child, you don't care much for the socio-economic backgrounds of your buddies. What impressed me as I walked into the school compound was a huge banyan tree near the entrance. But naturally, I didn't connect the banyan tree with enlightenment then.

As we got into the walled school compound, on the left was a playground and on the right was a long two-storey building with thick walls and wide corridors. The classrooms were big, with two large windows on the outer wall and two doors on the opposite side. In the nine classes that I went through ("studied" would be a little pretentious), there were never more than 40 students, and never fewer than 35. Apart from classrooms, what overwhelmed me was the enormous auditorium with sloping roofs, which was without columns. We assembled there for our daily prayer at seven, standing in long lines. Later, in that hall, I heard one of the most remarkable speeches in my life during an annual prize distribution ceremony. The speaker was Tarasankar Bandyopadhyay, the Bengali novelist and short-story writer. Much later, I would read his trilogy *Ganadevata (Divine Human)*, which I believe can be placed alongside the finest novels in world literature. The function happened shortly after the Second Indo-Pak War in 1965. Blackout had just been lifted, making it possible to organise the event. Tarasankar spoke on war and peace.

On the first day in the new school, I shared an unvarnished wooden desk for two with Sameer. As soon as we sat down, Sameer, who was one and a half times my size, kicked me on my leg. He went on kicking even as the teacher spoke, while I regretted the absence of feminine company of my previous school. I was far too timid to protest. Anyway, the budding he-man soon got bored with me and my inability to pick up a legitimate fight. He stopped kicking after a few hours and over time, became a somewhat condescending friend.

Sameer was a brilliant footballer. (Hence the urge to kick?) He used to play with much bigger boys of Class V, the senior class in the primary section, and even amongst them, he dribbled through any defence and scored whenever he wished to. We all expected Sameer to become a great footballer, but he ended up as a bank clerk, and I think, a union leader.

Those days, every parent believed formal education was the only path to success. Sports or creative arts were not considered a career option. As Sir Ken Robinson would famously say much later, children are made to go through school for 14 years because it takes that much time to destroy their creativity completely. But that has been changing in our generation. Many parents help their offspring's talents in sports to flourish, which has resulted in the long list of successful badminton and chess players and of course, cricketers from India.

I am absolutely certain that Sameer, had he been born in another country or in another time, he wouldn't have wasted his enormous talent in football in dusty ledgers and barren union rooms in a bank.

19| A Voyage of Discovery

The human mind is an incredible thing. It can conceive the magnificence of the heavens and the intricacies of the basic components of matter. Yet for each mind to achieve its full potential, it needs a spark. The spark of enquiry and wonder. ... Often, it comes from a teacher.[xix]
– Stephen Hawking

What first comes to my mind about my early schooling is the struggle to wake up in the morning, particularly in winters, in complete darkness. Ma would regularly carry a sleeping me and make me stand in the bathroom. I would wake up and start peeing the moment she ruthlessly splashed a mug of cold water on my feet.

As mom and I waited for the school bus under the portico of Basusree cinema, municipality workers would sweep and remove the previous day's detritus; then they would wash the road with foaming jets of untreated but clean Ganga water, for which separate pipelines had been laid across the city long ago. By the time we boarded the school bus, the city of my childhood would look like a freshly bathed beauty.

In winter, in the hour or so we got before school began, we played hide-and-seek in the early-morning fog that hung over the playground like a white blanket. The Nepali watchmen would light a fire with dry leaves and twigs and we would warm ourselves around it from time to time.

Our headmistress, Aparnadi, was very fair, beautiful, and had a shock of curly black hair. She smiled all the time and was never angry; we loved her, and at the same time, were scared of her. We had both men and women teachers. Elderly Ushadi was our music teacher when I joined school at Class III. Once she tried a chorus with all of us. With thirty boys singing Rabindranath Tagore's *Hold the touchstone of fire close to your heart* in about twenty-five different tunes on multiple scales, it must have been trying for poor Ushadi. I do not remember another music class when we all sang in chorus.

Although we weren't burdened with much homework, we were given weekly tests regularly, on Saturdays, which ensured I had a nodding acquaintance with text books. While handing back the test papers after correction, every teacher would ask us to add up the marks again. I do not know if it was a deliberate method to make us more confident children who would have in the back of their minds the experience of verifying what adults had done. No one would ever find a mistake. Only once I found I'd been awarded an extra mark, which I brought to the teacher's notice.

The teacher, I wish I could recall his name, reduced one mark and added it back to the total. He said, 'The extra mark is for your honesty.'

After this minor experiment with truth, for some time, my own biography continued parallel to that of the Father of the Nation. I was as average a student as Gandhi had been. But later ….

Physical punishments were rare. My only experience was when we had gone to the Bandel Church for a picnic. Anup and I went to explore an underground chamber in a dilapidated building there. Although we didn't find any buried treasure, the adventure was most satisfying. As we came out, Fate brought us face to face with our assistant headmaster, Khagen Babu. ….

One of my most memorable classroom experiences was when Amar Babu told us the story of Christopher Columbus's expedition to America.

> 'When Columbus saw neither land, nor a shore-based bird even after 28 days into the voyage', Amar Babu said, 'the crew became restive. Some of his sailors were convicted murderers. The Spanish Queen Isabella had released them from prison only because they had agreed to join the dangerous mission. Rations were running out; starvation and death stared the crew in the eyes. They were nervous and angry. The first mate had overheard some of them planning a mutiny … these murderers would stop at nothing. That evening, Columbus looked into the mist and endless gloom beyond the gunwale as an oil lamp swayed and threw light and darkness alternately … the sailors might kill him if

> he didn't give into their demand and turn back … the lamp was swaying … there was darkness and then there was light … he knew he was destined to be a man of history. He was the chosen one to discover an alternative sea route to India ….'

The teacher took a group of spellbound boys aboard Santa Maria.

20|"To Sir, with Love"

Education is what remains after one has forgotten what one has learned in school.
– Albert Einstein

This happened years ago. One morning, when I was cleaning the drawers of my writing desk, my friend Arunabha's visiting card popped up. He was in New Delhi then. The white business card with blue letters conjured up a strapping young boy before my eyes, stout in body and heart, always smiling. We had been in Class VII when Arunabha and I got into a nasty tangle with Umapati Babu, our Assistant Headmaster, an extraordinary gentleman.

My abiding memories of Umapati Babu go back to an afternoon when after weeks of incessant rains, the sun had come out bright and clear, and banks of fluffy white clouds were floating across an azure sky. Almost the entire school had got on to the slushy playground during the tiffin break, and innumerable football matches were being played on the same pitch simultaneously. The bell had announced the end of the recess, but there was something in the crisp autumn sun and the crystal sky that made the troop of muddy boys defy it. We went on playing; no one returned to classroom.

We were no angels, but such indiscipline was unthinkable even by our standards. After a few minutes, all of a sudden, there was a massive flight. Most of us didn't know what had caused the hasty and chaotic retreat, but a panic gripped us and we ran. The field emptied in minutes.

Then we noticed a familiar hefty figure standing beside the ground calmly, doing nothing. Meet Mr Umapati Bose, our Assistant Headmaster, who we called Umapati Babu.

The task of controlling and disciplining 800-odd young rowdies was left mainly to Umapati Babu. I don't think anyone else could have made such a daunting task look so utterly simple. A big man of dark complexion, he was seen only in a white kurta and a dhoti that scarcely covered his knees. He brooked no nonsense. Although he rarely raised his large hands to thrash an errant boy, his name spelled terror. And although Umapati Babu was synonymous with terror for us, he was revered in equal measure. I haven't come across another man who was so enormously feared and respected at the same time.

Dressed in the attire just described, Umapati Babu often scored goals from free kicks during the annual teacher-student football matches, although after so many decades, I am not quite sure if he could bend them like Beckham. Mostly busy with administrative work, Umapati Babu didn't teach any class regularly and no one knew what his fields of study were; but he could chip in anywhere when the situation demanded, and was equally at home in subjects ranging from Sanskrit to English to maths. In fact, the general belief among us, though may not be entirely accurate, was that he could step in for any teacher except for Maulvi Sir, who alone taught Urdu and Arabic, for which subjects there were no takers. Clean-shaven and always in smart European clothes, he looked a perfect antithesis of a Maulvi. (That such a dapper person was called a Maulvi shows how deep anti-Muslim prejudice ran in the Hindu Bengali's mind.)

One Saturday—on Saturdays our school worked half a day—we decided to play cricket after school. It was quite normal on Saturday afternoons, but to take out the cricketing gear, we had to get permission from the Assistant Headmaster. Incidentally, Arunabha and I went to Umapati Babu to get the clearance. By the time our game was over, the sports room had been locked. So, we left the cricket set on top of a cupboard in the teachers' room, which was the usual thing to do.

Come Monday, when Arunabha and I were summoned to the Assistant Head Master's room, we had no inkling that the stumps had been missing, or the misfortune that would follow for us. An epitome of simplicity and fair play, Umapati Babu bluntly accused us of stealing. Our mumbled protests were ignored, brushed aside, swatted like fleas. He closed the interview quickly: "Bring the stumps back before school begins tomorrow. But your troubles won't be over. We'll think about what to do next."

It was devastating. More than anything else, we wondered: How could Umapati Babu be so unfair? We were twelve or thirteen then, and we had faced injustice even earlier, but that incident brought home to us how cruelly unfair the world can be, an important lesson that everyone learns sooner or later.

The resolution of the crisis was a learning experience too. That afternoon, we begged and borrowed a few rupees to purchase a set of stumps. When we met Umapati Babu the next morning with the new stumps, for the first time in our young lives, we looked a figure of authority straight in the eyes and said, 'Sir, here is a set of new stumps. We haven't stolen anything. Never.'

Sir stared at us—eyes blazing—for what seemed an eternity. We cringed before the glare and knew our goose was cooked. Then his lineament softened and he said, 'Take your wretched stumps with you and get lost!'

To this day, I am not sure if I saw a hint of moistening in the eyes of the "tough guy", but I have little doubt it was his way of telling us that there is no shame in admitting one's mistake, even to a child.

* * *

As the incident ran before my eyes like a film, I sent an email to my friend, which ended with this sentence: 'So, Arunabha, we learned two invaluable lessons in quick succession, didn't we?'

Arunabha's reply came within hours. 'Yes,' he wrote in English, 'for me too, it was the first major brush with injustice. Since then, I've come across many such experiences, but there has always been one difference. Nobody owned up their mistakes like Umapati Babu did.'

I have told you I had sent an email to Arunabha that morning because I had suddenly discovered his visiting card. There was another reason too; Umapati Babu had passed away a few days before. If there is a God above, He seems to have forgotten the art of making men like Umapati Bose.

* * *

This has been a painful anecdote to write. A few months later, Arunabha too would leave us. Rest in peace, my friend.

21| A Reverse Roll-call

There is no system in the world, or any school in the country that's better than its teachers. Teachers are the life blood of the success of schools.[xx]
– Sir Ken Robinson

When we were promoted to Class VI, the half-sleeve white shirt remained the same, but the colour of our school shorts changed from white to khaki. We also moved to the secondary section of the school which began in the same premises at 11:00 in the morning. (The primary school got over at 10:30.)

I have just narrated the story of a distinguished gentleman and teacher we met in the secondary school: Umapati Bose. We had a number of other wonderful teachers. For example, Big Sunil Babu, who taught us English beautifully, together with dollops of affection. The qualifier Big has been used as there was a Small Sunil Babu too, who was much shorter. He was a brilliant and extremely hard-working maths teacher. Big Sunil Babu was always in dhoti, kurta, long socks, and covered shoes, for which reason he was also referred to as Sunil Babu in socks.

However, as Horace said, "Nihil est ab omni parte beatum," there are no unmixed blessings. Unlike in the primary section, not all the secondary section teachers got our unqualified admiration. I was in two minds whether to write about them because there is a saying in Bangla: Criticising a teacher is the worst possible sin. On the other hand, Syed Mujtaba Ali has shared this doggerel:

My guru might drink bootlegged liquor
But Nityananda Ray is *my* teacher.

So, it cuts both ways. After some hesitation, I have decided to describe the darker side too. For example, our first history teacher in the secondary school was the opposite of both Sunil Babus as far as energy was concerned. He would ask us to study a chapter at home and in the next class, we would have to reel out—one boy after the other—whatever we had managed to memorise, beginning at one end of the first bench. By the time the first speaker finished, the teacher would be snoring peacefully; the second student would pick up the baton. Every one of us would eagerly wait for Sudipto's turn to come, because he would speak from memory—on whatever the topic was, and sometimes beyond it—chapter(s) from Kiran Chowdhury's undergrad history textbook, every word of it. Sudipto would continue until the bell rang and so, when he began, we could indulge in whatever pastime we enjoyed, reading storybooks being a primary one. (We would graduate to pornography in due course, but that would be later.)

Sudipto had a memory that could be compared to the magnetic tape of the Grundig tape-recorder I was fortunate to see in action. His other intellectual faculties too matched his memory. He left the school two years later, when his father, an economics prof, took up a teaching job at a New Zealand university. Much later, thanks to another classmate Tushar, I spoke to Sudipto for a few minutes and then exchanged a couple of emails until he died in his early fifties. He was a professor at London School of Economics then. After his passing, I read Sudipto's breathtaking CV on the LSE website.

Academics was not my forte. Nor was I good at sports or music. I think the only area I was reasonably good at was painting. It is therefore natural that I would take the drawing lessons seriously. Our art teacher had come at the top of his class at Calcutta Government Art College. Much later, I would read a review of his (possibly only) painting exhibition in the Bangla magazine *Desh.* The critic wrote that school teaching had killed the artist in him; instead of an art teacher, he could have become a master artist.

To us it didn't matter how great a painter he was, but he thrilled us by quickly drawing brilliant landscapes in our drawing notebooks. He taught me how to use the oil pastel. I copied his style with reverence. When my oil pastel work at a sit-and-draw competition was judged the best in school, someone complained I had smuggled in one of the art teacher's landscapes and submitted it as my own work. Sadly, my idol too believed it was actually his work!

So, what I thought to be a great honour led to the ignominy of being labelled a cheat. After repeating the pastel drawing while the teacher sat in front, I told him, 'Sir, I won't accept the prize.'

The prize—which incidentally was sponsored by him—was a silver medal with his mother's name inscribed on it. He was taken aback by the cheeky protest and clearly, felt genuine remorse about his error of judgement. He also knew that in the land of Gandhi, I couldn't be punished for taking a moral high ground. After much melodrama over the next week or so, I was cajoled into accepting the medal.

I am not sure if I can find the medal now, but its memory stands for a lesson I've tried not to forget: to be fair, at least try to be fair, when I had the power over another human being, however small that power might have been. It also feels good that I was a pioneer in the field of "award-wapsi," long before it became a fashionable form of protest in India.

Patro Babu's speciality was a subject that is finer than fine arts: physics. He was easily the most exciting teacher we had in school. One had to be really dumb not to get a concept he explained. Besides teaching brilliantly, his other speciality was that he had worked out the physics of hitting errant boys in a way that maximum impact would be made with the least effort.

The redoubtable teacher had an unfortunate clash with Shakuntala Devi, who mesmerised the world by doing long arithmetical calculations (like multiplying two thirteen-digit numbers) in her head. The Wikipedia says at the University of California, Berkeley, she worked out the cube root of 61,629,875 and the seventh root of 170,859,375 under controlled conditions even before the psychologist who was testing her could jot down the numbers. (One of the reasons she could do it possibly was that she had had no formal education in her childhood. She was the daughter of a trapeze artist and a lion-tamer in a circus.)

When Shakuntala Devi visited our school, she was at the peak of her fame. We, all the high-school students, sat down on the floor of our auditorium, armed with results of long calculations in our notebooks which had been checked multiple times by multiple people. On stage, where Shakuntala Devi sat on an armless chair, there was a blackboard. A senior student would write down the task on the board and Shakuntala would give the answer almost before he could finish writing. The student who had prepared the task would confirm the result.

We were awe-struck, but not Patro Babu. He wrote a complex mathematical problem on the board, not a long arithmetical function. Shakuntala Devi hadn't claimed she could solve every mathematical problem under the sun. She looked at the blackboard and asked for the next task. To this, Patro Babu wrote on the board, "NOT solved". We were not impressed by the crude exhibition of vanity.

Vanity would be unthinkable about Shubhankar Babu, who taught chemistry. Another excellent teacher, he would not only not hit anyone, he wouldn't raise his voice ever. That doesn't mean our stupidity and lack of application didn't hurt him. But for him, the most violent form of admonition was a wry smile.

Although I studied science in high school, I was most impressed by three English teachers: Suprabhat Babu, Ajit Babu, and Sailesh Babu. Apart from being exceedingly well-read, each one of them was a minor rock star; there was never a dull moment when they were in class. Ajit Babu directed three of us in a play based on the Irish Independence struggle: Lady Augusta Gregory's *The Rising of the Moon.* It was an unforgettable experience.

Suprabhat Babu, who genuinely loved us, would hit the ceiling often. And every time that happened, we felt he might suffer a stroke. One day, when someone did something abominable, Sir started from a corner. Standing menacingly in front of the first desk, he asks, 'Did you do it?' Student 1 stands up: 'No, Sir.' Sir (at the top of his voice): 'Are you sure?' Without waiting for an answer, Suprabhat Babu lands three hefty blows on the fellow and moves on to next in line, 'Did you do it?' Boy 2: 'No Sir.' Three smacks and then to the next person. The same words and action were repeated until the teacher was completely exhausted. I haven't seen a more even-handed distribution of justice. The people who abolished corporal punishment in schools had no idea how entertaining it could be with teachers like Suprabhat Babu around. During the rest of our school days, if we wished to hit a classmate, we wouldn't forget to ask 'Are you sure?' before the action.

Ramaranjan Adhikary, who taught us Bangla, had a whacky sense of humour. He regaled us with his wit even when he taught grammar. Thanks to him, we learned grammar could be genuinely entertaining. And maybe, because of him, I would later try to write an unintimidating book on English Grammar!

Ramaranjan Babu passed away in May 2019. Umapati Babu and Suprabhat Babu had left earlier. And surely, some others too would have gone. But they continue to live in our collective memory. Some teachers are like parents. They continue to live after their death.

22| A Gift of Misery

The most fantastic gift I ever received was also the cause of one of the greatest miseries I ever suffered. The story began when I went to Bareilly in Uttar Pradesh to spend a week with an aunt, my mom's oldest sister Purnima. I was around 12 then.

Before moving on to the story, let me introduce my aunt to you. Everyone in my mom's family was technologically challenged. (More about it later.) But Aunt Purnima's fear of anything mechanical went beyond absurdity. She couldn't dial a telephone, although she could give you an extempore speech on mind and consciousness.

While her husband, an army officer, was posted to Madras, she did her Masters in History. I believe she was on the wrong side of fifty then. Later, she taught at a college in Ooty. In the course of time, she became the principal of the college. I am giving you her short CV because you'll need the background to appreciate the story that follows.

Once she was on a college bus on her way home along with students. The vehicle broke down on the way. Fortunately, there was a house with a telephone nearby, from where they could call the office to ask for another vehicle. The driver requested her to talk to the office as she was the only person on the bus who had the authority to order the admin guys at college. But, how could she? She couldn't dial a telephone!

So, she wrapped herself tightly with her shawl and pretended to have suddenly taken ill.

I guess the transition from a homemaker to a college prof wasn't difficult for her otherwise because she was a passionate reader. She was also a brilliant conversationalist and cook. I saw both Jiddu Krishnamoorthy and Tarla Dalal in her kitchen and she would read them alternately, holding a book in her left hand, even as she stirred a pot.

Although her approach to cooking seemed causal, her dishes were exquisite. And they looked perfect too. Her vegetable cutlets seemed machine-made. Did it matter that she couldn't make a phone call?

Moving back in time to Bareilly, where her husband had been posted, it happened during the summer vacation when their son, who was studying at a boarding school, had been home. I was astonished to see the picture-postcard neatness of the cantonment: its wide, parallel roads lined with eucalyptus trees, smartly dressed jawans in starched bottle-green uniform riding green Atlas bicycles, bungalows that seemed straight out of story books. They even had chimneys! Everything about the place was wonderful. I was puzzled by the fact that without exception, trunks of all the trees in the cantonment were painted white up to a height of say four feet. Who did it, and why?

When I asked my cousin, he said airily, 'Well, it's one of the basic rules of the Indian army: jawans paint everything stationery and salute everything moving.'

Another wonder for me—it wasn't unmixed with envy—was my cousin's sporting kit. He had a cabinet full of cricket bats and balls, stumps, hockey sticks, badminton rackets and a solitary football, which lay at the bottom, deflated, unloved, and abandoned.

Such a treasure trove was unimaginable for me, and without a shadow of a doubt, for any of my classmates. Even a football was a luxury for us. In the free periods in school, we generally played football with small rubber balls.

The day before we were to leave Bareilly, when Aunt asked me what I would like to have as a gift, I felt just as the sages from our mythology would have felt when—after a long and sadistic penance—benevolent gods asked them to name the boon they wished to have. For me, there weren't too many things to choose from: it could either be a cricket bat or a football. Which one? Chandu Borde or Chuni Goswami?

In the end, it was a brand-new fully-grown Size 5 football!

Back home, it instantly raised my street cred. I was a minor hero, perhaps the only individual owner of a real football in school. Among friends I suddenly became someone who had to be treated with a little respect. I started enjoying my days under the sun.

Two days later, I left the football behind under my desk while leaving school. I realised my mistake soon after reaching home and rushed back with my friend Swadesh.

The imposing iron gate of our school had been locked and the shadow of the banyan tree in the compound had spread far; our conscientious Gurkha guard refused to let us in. Swadesh and I begged, but not a line moved on his impassive face.

After some time, when he saw me in tears, his heart melted. We ran to the classroom … Not a speck of dust had shifted in the room since when we had left it, except that there was no sign of the ball. An undreamt dream had come true without my asking, and I lost it all because of carelessness. It was devastating. The world crumbled around me in the forlorn classroom.

As I was leaving the school compound, rays of the setting sun met my eyes and something happened within me. Deep within, I felt a football was not something worth being upset about. Life was bigger.

The most fantastic gift I ever received was also the cause of perhaps the most miserable hour in my life. And the lesson, like all important lessons in life, had to be learned through pain.

That afternoon, I learned that happiness and sorrow are two sides of the same coin, and in the end, neither really matters.

23| Friendship Therapy

Fighting has always been, more or less, a form of blindness.[xxi]
– José Saramago

Academically, Rahul was one of the best in our reasonably strong class. He always came at or near the top. Like all budding Bengali intellectuals, Rahul was thin, wore specs, and avoided contact sports like football or boxing. If that gave you the picture of a boring bespectacled bookworm, you would be wrong. Rahul was charming, ever smiling, had no airs about his considerable academic ability, and was loved by all. And he preferred the last bench, unlike most "good" students.

When we were in Class IX, Rahul and I sat side by side across an aisle on the last row. It was the final period of the day. Like any normal fourteen-year-old, we looked forward to hearing the final bell, and looked at the sky and the mellow light outside, sitting on wooden benches that had been living trees long ago in which birds would build nests.

For some reason, Rahul was in a particularly mischievous mood that afternoon. Every time the teacher, Adwaita Babu turned towards the blackboard, he would pick up a piece of broken chalk—he had saved a neat pile of them—and throw it at me. I threw it back, dutifully. We both were enjoying this little game on the side of an algebra lesson.

Teachers can see through the back of their head, a quality that some people mistakenly call the sixth sense. Adwaita Babu gave us a dirty look or two, but said nothing. Towards the end of the class, as I returned Rahul's last missile, Adwaita Babu turned suddenly and caught me in action. (But naturally, he hadn't seen the first part of the act.)

The teacher calmly walked towards me and without wasting time on preliminaries, pulled me up by the collar gave me a solid thrashing in the limited time available before EOD, as my friends watched intently with shades of emotions ranging from genuine sympathy to uninhibited glee. It was aeons before corporal punishment was banned in schools and our wonderful teachers had to resort to this time-tested technique to control the bunch of young hooligans under their tutelage. We considered an occasional manhandling by our able-bodied male teachers as much a part of our boys-only school as was the beautiful banyan tree at its entrance. We took it in our stride, without complaint, almost gracefully.

So, when the class ended, I felt no ill will towards the Adwaita Babu, but thought it would be a good idea to pass on what I had got to Rahul, because of two important reasons. First, it was he who had started it; second and more important, he was even thinner than me. So instead of leaving the classroom, I tapped him on the shoulder and invited him to a duel. Rahul, who was a sport, accepted the challenge happily. Both of us took off our glasses. Friends helped, by moving desks to construct a makeshift arena. (Recently, as I watched the opening scene of Aamir Khan's film *Dangal*, I recalled our fight.)

Surprisingly, he gave me a tough fight and pushed me to a corner, hitting me repeatedly utilising the reach offered by his thin, long arms. I regretted my decision to engage him in combat, but hung on grimly. … Suddenly, I managed to land a good right jab on the left of Rahul's face. My friend and adversary bent down in excruciating pain, cupping his left eye. I won on TKO, much against the flow of the contest.

Rahul didn't come to school the next day. And he couldn't take the annual exam shortly thereafter—not because of the injury, but because of some illness. So, we were never in the same class again. I graduated from school a year before him and we didn't meet for decades.

The victory in the skirmish gave me no pleasure. I felt miserable to have hurt a good soul and I carried a sense of guilt that time didn't heal. The normal thing to do would have been to go to him and apologise. I thought of it, but being the stupid oaf I was, I never got round to doing it. Or maybe, apologising seems too theatrical when you are 14 or 15.

* * *

Much later, maybe after 30 years, another friend Dipankar and I were sauntering around in Kolkata on a Sunday evening when he said, 'We're near Rahul's home. Shall we barge in?'

Those days, I was suffering from frequent bouts of backache. Non-steroidal anti-inflammatory drugs (NSAIDs) gave some temporary relief—but doctors said they also chewed up the kidney. So, most of the time, I suffered in silence. That evening too, I had a nasty backache. The pain—which would have been at 8 on a scale of 1 to 10—had the tenacity of a fascist. When Dipankar suggested we meet Rahul, I'd been thinking of taking a taxi home.

But I grabbed the opportunity with both hands. As we were crossing Vivekananda Park, electricity failed, plunging the area into darkness, opening up the starry sky. As I looked up, my mind too was enveloped in darkness. The pain had become rather unbearable … I could barely walk.

Rahul was at home. In the course of our chat, I managed to slip in the line that I had wanted to say for decades, 'Rahul, I've felt terrible ever since that day. But I've never got round to telling you. …'

Rahul instantly knew what day I was talking about. He cut me short, 'Yes, I thought you had made chutney of my left eyeball … couldn't see with the eye for a few days and couldn't tell my parents either ….' He said this as if he was recalling a particularly happy moment of his childhood and broke into a hearty laughter.

* * *

The litmus test of whether an old friendship is alive or not happens when you meet an old pal after a long time. If you have nothing to talk, if you have to hunt for common topics, you know that the friendship is dead. If that happened, you must say you have to buy an injection for your mom-in-law and buzz off quickly. However, that evening, although the three of us had followed completely different trajectories in life and although I was meeting Rahul for the first time after leaving school, I felt I was picking up the thread after a week's gap. We went on talking until late into the evening and parted reluctantly, with lots of notes put aside to be compared the next time.

As Dipankar and I were walking towards the bus stop, I suddenly realised I had no back pain. None at all!

24| Value of Education?

One day, [Teacher Debu] came across a doggerel in a children's textbook, "Study well. As a matter of course, / You'll drive a car, ride a horse." Debu struck off the lines repeatedly. Then he wrote on the black board: "Study well; you will see, / One and all respect thee."
– Tarasankar Banerjee

Upper-caste Bengalis have always been unenthusiastic about manual work. In my childhood, middleclass Bengali parents believed education was the only path to salvation for their offspring. Consequently, we grew up hearing the ridiculous doggerel that the Bengali novelist Tarasankar rejected in his seminal novel *Ganadebata* (Part 1, Chapter 11). Please see the epigraph above.

In reality, most highly educated people not only didn't drive cars or ride horses, many of them lived in penury. I saw one such person from close quarters: my kaku, Dad's younger brother Subimal, who lived from hand to mouth, to use a cliché. Let me narrate his story here.

Subimal Sinha had studied well; he could teach college students an assortment of subjects: Bangla, English, Maths, Commerce, Economics and maybe, Botany. He had graduated in Botany from Calcutta University. (Subimal had been a good student, but he tried to copy at a university exam to win a bet. Consequently, he lost an academic year. My dad met the Vice-Chancellor, the redoubtable Sir Ashutosh Mukherjee CSI FRAS FRSE MRIA, to avoid greater punishment to his younger brother.) Following this, Subimal acquired two Master's degrees, I believe, in Economics, and Bangla; he also read for entertainment. In the decent library at his sparsely furnished Bhawanipur flat, I saw three volumes of well-thumbed, *Das Kapial* with underlines and profuse notes on the margins, although he hated Marxism. Besides books, he had a large well-preserved collection of empty cartons of soaps, toothpastes, electric bulbs, etc.—which occupied half the long balcony in his spacious three-room flat.

If nobody asked Subimal why he collected trash so methodically, it was perhaps because everyone around was scared of his acerbic tongue. Once he told a middle-aged younger cousin of his, 'A trained police dog has more brains than you.' When a niece who had just joined an undergrad course in economics went to seek his blessings, he said in a matter-of-fact way, 'Good that you are starting economics honours, but you aren't going to complete it.' The uncle's prophesy failed, the niece did exceedingly well in life!

His appearance too was rather forbidding. Tallish and extremely slender, he had a jungle of unkempt hair, moustache, and beard through which a pair of bright eyes cast a piercing glance at his interlocutor through thick bifocal glasses. As children, Ruby and I feared him like nobody else. But my mother, who used to get on with everyone, had an amicable relationship with him. Kaku too respected her and would bend down to touch her feet whenever there was an occasion, much to the discomfort of Mother, who was seven years his younger (but senior to him on the family pyramid). Although they didn't meet often, Kaku used to write letters to his sister-in-law on postcards. In a beautiful hand, he filled every millimetre of the postcard with quotidian descriptions of his unusual life.

Uncle cooked and did all the housework himself, without any help. When grandma spent her sightless last few years with him, she was looked after by an elderly woman, Bamun di. *Bamun* is a synonym of *Brahmin* in Bangla. Her name was an illustration that caste-names sometimes became proper nouns those days.

Kaku had been a college teacher before Partition. Since he left East Pakistan, he didn't take up—maybe he didn't find—another job. His life-long work was offering private tuitions at home which fetched him enough to meet his modest needs. But he had only a few students maybe because not many were robust enough to withstand his insults.

Besides reading and teaching, Subimal Sinha specialised in preserving food. Although he didn't have a refrigerator—which anyway was hardly seen in middle-class homes—he preserved cooked food sometimes for six months by heating it every day. His letters to mom would typically contain lines like this:

> "I bought a large koi fish on 7 December last year and cooked it on the same day. Following my own methods, I preserved it and ate it on 7 June. The fish was absolutely fine."

Needless to say, his relations were scared of being offered cooked food in his home! Incidentally, not all his experiments were successful. Once he had to be hospitalised for a severe stomach disorder. A few weeks later, he wrote to mom:

> Respected Boudi,
>
> Pranam. Nobody except me knows what caused my recent illness. I wish to make a confession.
>
> Actually, on 30 August 1945, I stole 10 grams of potassium cyanide from the laboratory of the college I was then teaching at. Recently, when I decided to end my life, I consumed it. But unfortunately, either the cyanide had been contaminated or the sample had lost its potency during the 40 years of heat and humidity. So my mission failed and I had to suffer the ignominy of spending a fortnight in a dirty hospital. …

This prosaic and unconventional uncle of mine fell in love with a much younger female student of his when he was pushing fifty and she was half his age; they got married despite strong disapproval of both the families. (I added the qualifier female in deference to today's sensibilities, but in the 1960s, same-sex marriage was unimaginable.) The dissimilar couple had a girl child. In order to bring up the baby properly, Kaku memorised Dr Spock's *Baby and Child Care.* Much later, when my daughter was little, he would telephone my wife Arundhati and tell her what to do when, including mentioning the page number of Dr Spock's book.

Although Kaku and Kakima's love story didn't end happily, Kaku kept reading through marital discord and financial troubles. He even wrote a treatise on the Theory of Evolution—rather curiously—in 112 ten-line verses. (His training in botany would have helped!) Here is Verse 31 from his never-sold book *Fare Well, Life!*

Such unicellular life of many diverse kinds
Upon the earth's surface the microbiologist finds;
Which may have continued unchanged until today;
Or may have changed only imperceptibly, say
Protophyta and *Protozoa* by name,
The first plants and the first animals, almost the same
But within such distinction as we did mention,
That the former inorganic matter does feed on,
While the latter must have for their victual
Either some plant or some other animal.

He used to brag, I hope in jest, he was greater than Darwin because the original genius hadn't been able to write his theory in English verse despite being a native speaker of English!

* * *

After seeing my own uncle, I had strong reasons not to believe in any correlation between education and wealth. In fact, like me, lots of people had serious doubts about the saying above; it had another version:

Study well. As a matter of course,
You'll be trampled by a carriage horse.

But on the whole, despite its somewhat iffy prospects, education was considered important and not necessarily subservient to financial motives. In fact, many believed education was valuable because it made one a better human being. I can confidently say that people in general believed "knowledge" was valuable in itself.

That was starkly different from the situation half a century later, when most people don't see the point of acquiring knowledge that doesn't lead to material benefit. In fact, a lot of people these days believe abstract knowledge must be avoided at all costs, like unplanned pregnancy.

My father was fond of quoting a Sanskrit saying: *A king is worshipped in his own kingdom, but a learned man is worshipped everywhere.* But Baba's commitment to learning did not translate into his son becoming a good student: I was never more than halfway up my class. However, my sister and I were not under constant pressure to excel in studies. It would be significant to note that my family wasn't exceptional in this regard. A Bengali scholar, who was scholar enough to be worshipped everywhere, Rabindra Kumar Dasgupta (1915-2009) wrote[xxii]:

> [When we were children,] no parent tried to make supermen out of their offspring. Some visitors to our house would ask me what I would become after growing up. I didn't know how to respond to them. One day, I asked my father, 'What will I be when I grow up?' He said, 'There's no need to think about it now.' I said that some of our guests asked me the question. He said, 'Tell them you'll be a vegetable vendor.' I did not think it was a strange proposition. Since then when someone asked 'What will you be when you grow up?', I responded, 'I'll sell vegetables.'

My continued inability to do well in studies did not unnerve my parents. Consequently, we had a lot of space for fun and frolic, unlike the gadget-rich-time-poor middle-class children today, whose evenings are often spent in trips from one tuition centre to another. Besides enjoying freedom and friendships, we were privileged to go on longish vacations once in a way, particularly during the month-long summer and autumn holidays.

25| Another Time, through Another Pair of Eyes

Aunt Helena (who Ruby and I call Mashima) and Ma studied together at a primary school. Since then, they have been friends. I think she is Ma's best friend. Every week, they exchange postcards. Every bit of the space in those postcards is filled out.

We have just come back after spending a week at Mashima's home in a village. Here is what I have written in my diary about her family, their dog, and their beautiful village Chapra.

24 December: As soon as the train began to move, Ruby and I stood up on our seat by the window, clutched the window bars and looked out. There were two rows of seats along the two sides of the coach. And there was another long seat along the middle with a common backrest. On that, people sat back-to-back. We were on a window seat facing east. I know because the sun was still rising (the train started at 7). As the train picked up speed, trees, houses, men, women, bazaars, roads, and stray dogs rushed past us even as they stood still. I hadn't seen anything like that before. It was as amazing as hearing Mother's voice through a radio for the first time.

That day, Ma was telling the story of the War of Troy. I was sure that somehow, she had become very small and got into the radio, just as the Greek soldiers had got into the wooden horse. I looked through the grille behind the radio, but didn't see her. Ma has given several radio talks later, and every time, I found it amazing. I am no longer small, but even now, I don't understand how it happens. I asked Baba about it, but what he said didn't make sense.

Ruby and I kept standing like that, with our back to other passengers, but we had to bend down every now and then when bits of coal got into our eyes. Ma removed them by rolling a corner of her sari into a soft twig.

After a few hours, we got off at a station called Krishnanagar. Then we got onto a blue Bedford bus. (My school has a green Bedford.) It was crowded. Many things were written inside in Bengali: "Don't put your hand outside"; "Don't spit inside"; "Beware of pickpockets"; "Company is not responsible for your goods" (Who is Company?); "Put children on your lap"; "No change for five- and ten-rupee notes". There were many people on the bus, and a goat.

After some time, the conductor came and told Ma that we could go to the "First Class" section if we wanted to. So, we got off and boarded the bus again through the front door and sat behind the driver. A wire mesh separated us from the rest of the bus.

The bus went through uneven fields on which there was nothing. Ma said paddy had just been cut and taken away; so there was nothing on the fields. In some places, we came across large fields of yellow flowers. The bus stopped several times on the way. Finally, our journey ended at a marketplace called Haat Chapra, which had stores on both sides of the road. But they looked different from the stores in Calcutta, which is the capital of the state of West Bengal.

Two boys were waiting for us. One was just a few years older than me, but the other was much bigger. He was in Class VIII. The smaller boy is Mithuda and the bigger one, Babulda. I am calling them dadas, but actually, I hadn't met them before. They were Aunt Helena's sons. Babulda put our bags on the carrier of his cycle, tied them with a rope, and pushed it along. Mithuda said he comes to the market often to see buses crossing Haat Chapra every half an hour or so. (Both of them can ride bicycles. Will they teach me?)

Helena Mashima, Mesomoshai, their daughter Alodi, and a big brown dog Tiger welcomed us. Tiger is very friendly. Uncle said all the thieves of the village are scared of Tiger; they never visit their house. Auntie gave us cold water in brass tumblers. The tumbler was so fat that I had to hold it with both hands.

Their house is not like the other houses in the village. It is a big one-storey pink building made of bricks. To enter the house, you have to climb a few stairs to reach a wide veranda. In the veranda, there is a calendar with Jesus Christ's picture on the wall, and a long wooden bench with a back-rest, somewhat like the seat in the middle in the railway coach. Right across the road is a school. Above the main entrance to the school, it was written "King Edward Boys' School Estd. 1852" (Babulda told me the meaning of "Estd.") Beside the house, there is a huge open field with many trees. In the middle of the field is a big white church. Behind the church is a burial ground. Christians put their dead in boxes and bury them.

Behind the house is an orchard with hundreds of tall leafy trees. Uncle said there was a big beehive in the garden. We should not go near it. (Bees are dangerous.) Auntie cooks in a thatched hut beside the main house. We ate there, sitting on the floor. The rice looked different from the rice we eat at home. It was reddish and the grains were much fatter; it tasted good. The pickle made of kul was great. A rack in Mashima's kitchen has a row of jars containing many different pickles. She offered us only one of them today.

After we had food, we went to the orchard behind the house. There were many mango and guava trees in the orchard, but there were no mangoes. The place is a little dark even in daytime. For the first time in my life, I climbed a tree. It was a small tree. In Bangla, we call the fruit safeda. We sat on the tree and ate safeda. They were ripe, juicy, and very sweet.

25 December: It has been a busy day. In the morning, we heard the sound of a gong every few minutes. Then we all went to the church. Babulda, Mithuda and Alodi were in new clothes. If you go inside a church, you will find it is actually a big hall, with a stage at the far end. A priest in a long white robe stands there. Behind him are a big cross, a statue of Jesus, and many candles on large shining brass candle stands. On one side is a platform. It is for the church singers. There are many desks and wooden benches in the church. Do they also hold classes there?

The prayers and all the songs were in Bangla. The best part of Christmas was the roasted chicken that Mashima prepared in the evening. It was yummy!

26 December: Yesterday, a big fair begun on the field behind King Edward Boys' School (Estd. 1852). Many temporary stores have been set up with bamboo and tarpaulin. They are selling fried snacks, sweets, household utensils, agricultural tools, clothes, and knick-knacks for decorating homes.

The more interesting part of the fair is where the merry-go-rounds and a Ferris wheel are. A ride in either of them costs ten naya paise. There is also a circus tent and a magician's tent. In another tent, you can get your photograph taken.

Yesterday went quickly. There are so much to see in the fair. When I went to bed, I was dying to get up in the morning and go back to the fairground.

27 December: I love the Ferris wheel the most, although it is scary and I get a strange feeling in my stomach when the basket tumbles down. My next favourite is shooting air guns. In the afternoon, I spent all my cash recklessly and had no money for the Ferris wheel. As I stood before the Ferris wheel and watched it, a gentleman gave me a two-anna coin. I took it and took a ride. When I told Ma about this, she became angry, needlessly. After all, I didn't ask him to give me anything!

31 December: I have been very busy during the last few days. Although Baba asked me to jot down what happened every day, I couldn't write anything after the 27th. In the evening, when I had to sit down for writing, I felt too tired.

Every morning during the last few days, there were contests where farmers placed their flowers, vegetables, cows, and goats before judges. Aunt Helena got a prize for a potted dahlia plant, and uncle got the prize for the biggest pumpkin in the show. There were also huge ash gourds and aubergines.

In the evenings, the fairground came alive with magicians, jugglers and talking dolls under Petromax lights. (I forgot to say: there is no electricity in Chapra.) The magic show was no good. Babulda could figure out most of the tricks. But how did the doll talk? How did it understand the questions asked by the audience?

We went to the fair all by ourselves. In a village, things are different. Children go around without an adult watching over them all the time. I didn't cry when we left.

26| Ah! The Taj?

No one can say beforehand what among their childhood experiences will be retained, and what will be erased forever. There is no rule that tells us what we will remember and what we won't. That is the magic about memory[xxiii]

- Satyajit Ray

In my early childhood, the most famous and happening places our family visited were Agra and Bombay. I loved those trips, but if I were to rank my childhood holidays, visits to Aunt Helena's home in a dusty, unglamorous village would easily figure at the top. Also, I have practically no recollection of the Fatehpur Sikri Fort. Neither was the visit to the Taj my most exciting experience there. I'll come back to it in a moment.

My parents were fond of a younger cousin of my dad, who Ruby and I called Shyamal Kaku. While we were in that uncle's home in Agra, we never felt we were guests. Uncle loved us, and his wife too was an epitome of affection. My mom, sister, and I went to Agra first and dad joined us a few days later.

Dad didn't believe in travelling light. One morning, he got off a tonga, that is, a one-horse two-wheel hackney carriage, along with a large trunk, a small bag (with his shaving kit etc.), a big earthen pot (drinking water supply for the long train journey), and his constant companion, a stout valve radio with a black Bakelite body packed in a cardboard box. After considerable efforts and with uncle's help, Dad even managed to fix a make-shift arial across uncle's courtyard for his weeklong stay in Agra.

Shyamal Kaku, Jharna Kakima, their new-born daughter, and one of uncle's younger sisters Nelie Pishi lived in an old building that looked quite different from the houses in Calcutta. The house and its treeless cemented courtyard were surrounded by solid high walls on four sides. A few sparsely-furnished circular domed rooms close to the rear wall served as the living quarters. The rooms had incredibly thick walls with tiny little windows. A stout wooden door on the outer wall connected the house to the rest of the world. The architecture pointed at a time when the women had to be kept hidden from the world's polluting gaze. Rich people's homes would then have separate quarters which were closed to outsiders, the zenana. But for ordinary folks, the entire house had to be zenana.

The near absence of windows didn't matter. The family spent most of its time in the open courtyard. The pleasantly warm October sunlight poured on us like happiness.

When I think back of the hexagonal structures with a dome on top, I feel maybe, they were hundreds of years old. Did a minion of Emperor Shah Jahan live there once? Had it borne footsteps of people who lived in a very different time in a very different world?

The finest aspect of the house was its location. From there, the Taj Mahal was a just a short walk along narrow alleys on which tongas were the main mode of transport. That my uncle's office was in the Taj Mahal complex was a big bonus. He was the manager of a store that sold handicrafts from Bengal, a rather modest store called "West Bengal State Handicrafts Emporium" or something equally pompous.

My sister and I almost lived in the Taj Mahal complex during the day. Soon after breakfast, we sprinted to the Taj; we went there in the afternoons too. There were no entry tickets. We ran round the fountains and manicured flower beds freely, lost ourselves in the halls and chambers of the mausoleum, and I would jump off its low terraces. If subsequent memory hasn't turned it into a palimpsest, the Yamuna was nearly dry even then. But I certainly didn't care much for her.

Neither did I admire the architecture of the Taj, or its aesthetics. And needless to say, I was too young to care for the mushy regal love story behind the monument. It was a closed structure that was almost as big as any open space! And that was about all.

As a matter of childhood fact, I found the making of malai a lot more interesting than the Taj. There were several dimly lit sweetmeat shops nearby. They had basic wooden tables and long benches for customers and an open fire burning bright in one corner. A flaccid bare-bodied man with a big paunch would keep fanning with a hand fan the milk boiling in an enormous wok set upon an equally big oven. As thick layers of cream formed on the milk, I stood transfixed in front of the shop and watched the spectacle! But no one in our house ever bought the malai. I must go back to Agra one day to taste what I believed was an absolutely heavenly stuff!

27| Bombay by the Arabian Sea

The Taj might have failed to impress me, the Arabian Sea didn't.

Father wasn't with us on our trip to Bombay, where we stayed with an uncle of my mom—who incidentally was only a little older than her. They were evidently good friends. The smallish flat in Dadar was well-organised. The beds, sofas, dining table with a spotless table cloth and possibly table mats, everything seemed perfectly arranged and—I now think—colour-coordinated. Just outside the dining room was a balcony from where a fascinated me watched streams of cars, mostly made-in-India Fiats, on the smooth wide road below. Compared to what I saw from our second-floor flat in Calcutta, the men and vehicles looked bigger, unless memory is playing tricks with me. So I guess we were on the first floor. The road below was a picture of an efficient city, people went about their business silently. I also saw something for the first time in their home: towels with the letter "G" embroidered on it. I guessed G stood for guests.

There was a girl and a boy in the family. Bubuda and his younger sister Buṛidi. They were older than Ruby and me. Bombay then was the undisputed capital of Indian cricket and Bubuda, who was in high school, was a budding cricketer. He told me Ramakant Desai, the only fast bowler of the Indian cricket team of the time, had come to his school once. (I had seen Desai in action at the Eden Gardens in Calcutta, a fast bowler under five and a half feet who could generate tremendous pace for his small frame. He was, and possibly has been, the shortest fast bowler in the history of test cricket.) Our young host said that like every other batsman in his school team, he had faced one ball from Desai and had felt a tremendous jolt when the ball hit his bat. This impressive story put him on a pedestal for me.

Fifty years ago, Bombay was more distant from Calcutta than Mumbai is from Kolkata today. We lost touch with the wonderful family and I would never meet my childhood hero again.

What fascinated me most about the city were the clean wide roads and the long array of uniformly tall (possibly four-storeyed) buildings in Dadar. At least that is the image that has been etched in my head permanently. Bombay looked very much like the cityscapes seen on movie posters: rectangular façades of similar buildings with evenly spaced windows on flat walls. This aspect of the city, i.e. long lines of rectangular blocks, hadn't changed much when I visited the place again in the 1980s. During that trip, the city revived my childhood wonder: how do people find their own homes when they get back from office? The question came to my mind perhaps because of my own experience of finding Buṛidi's house once, a story I am going to tell you in a minute.

Besides the cityscape, what I found fascinating were the red BEST buses. They were clean, red, and efficient, just like the CSTC buses back home. But unlike Calcutta, people didn't jostle and fight and elbow each other to board buses. They stood in queues and patiently waited for their turn to get on; they also bought tickets before taking a seat. Later, whenever I travelled to Mumbai, I found that neither the BEST bus nor the Arabian Sea had changed. I wish I could say the same thing about the public buses of Kolkata. Maharashtra hasn't suffered the economic and social decline that West Bengal has experienced in the last 50 years. Mercifully, they never had a communist government ever.

During the trip, one of mom's colleagues accompanied us, but stayed elsewhere. One morning, she accompanied us when we took a bus to see the sea. We got off at the bus terminus way beyond the city limits, at a place called Juhu. We began walking towards the sea. After covering quite a distance in the blazing sun, we began wondering if we were on the right track. The spotlessly clean roads were empty and the picture-postcard bungalows on either side clearly belonged to another world. There was no one who we could ask for directions.

Suddenly, as we turned a corner, I saw a vast endless something that was making a guttural growl. I hadn't seen a sea before, and before I knew what it was, it dragged me like a powerful magnet. I forgot everything and ran, leaving my mother, her friend, and sister behind.

For some time, as sand glistened under my feet, I stood transfixed before the enormity of the ocean. It was one of those rare moments when we face the grandeur of Nature for the first time, and forget everything else irrespective of our age or life experience.

My mind, which had gone numb, was woken up when my mother's colleague boxed my ear with all her might for my intransigence of running away. She was a teacher and an NCC instructress to boot. Brooked no indiscipline. The public humiliation hurt, but it didn't dampen my spirit. For many years since that morning, I closed my eyes and tried to recreate that sense of awe and wonder of my first tête-à-tête with the sea.

* * *

The day before we were to leave, I went out to buy something from a store which was just round the corner. While returning, I thought I knew the way home and walked on. But soon I realised I was lost. As I wandered in Dadar, each one of the thousands of buildings of similar heights looked the same. In my efforts to get back, I only managed to get away from my destination. With every passing moment, I was moving farther and farther away from Ma; I was getting lost in a static sea of imposing buildings.

After half an hour or so, Buṛidi rescued me from a place half a mile away. During the half an hour that has been etched firmly in my head, I wasn't scared, however improbable it might sound.

Perhaps losing oneself is not such a bad idea after all. We just don't give it a try!

28| Journeys to Nowhere

Rigid iron was sleeping, lifeless
We have woken him up ...
We have ended his silence for ages,
He does what we ask him to.
Static before, now he runs keenly
To win the world,
And we hold the reins without fear.[xxiv]
– Rabindranath Tagore

If you haven't visited Kolkata during the winter, please go there at least once between December and February. Nowhere else does the sky take on a more perfect shade of blue, nowhere else will you find crispier air, tastier oranges, lovelier dahlias, or yummier plum cakes (from Nahoum's in New Market). By the way, Nahoum's was a humble bakery run by a Baghdadi Jewish family that has turned into a landmark in the city. The original owners have moved on to Australia and the other world; the bakery is now run by their relations and Muslim employees. (If you raised your brow after reading my statement about oranges and dahlias, a writer is entitled to his fancies, isn't he? But I am serious about the plum cake!)

For us, winters also meant a terrace garden with white chrysanthemums and yellow-orange marigolds in flowerpots. Baba tended the garden all by himself, often sitting on a wicker stool. He would get the seeds, saplings, and composted soil from the Horticultural Society nursery in Alipore. Thin men in meagre clothes would bring the soil in handcarts and climb up to our third-floor terrace with large sacks on their backs. At the annual Horticultural Society flower show, we would be stunned by enormous dahlias and the variety of roses.

Besides the flower show, other mandatory activities during winters used to be a visit to the zoo, and occasionally, a circus show. But even more exciting than a circus was the magician PC Sorcar. By the way, Sarkar is a common Bengali surname, but no other Sarkar I know spells it as Sorcar. I guess the great magician wished to relate his name to sorcery? (Let me add that the Late PC Sorcar's son, "Junior PC Sorcar", performs all the tricks his father did with equal self-assurance to regale the next generation of audience. "Junior" can vanish trains as a matter of course, it seems. And once he vanished the Victoria Memorial for his audience, I am told!)

Of the many PC Sorcar tricks that flabbergasted me, one was the X-Ray eyes. Sorcar would invite members of the audience to come on stage and check a dough of flour. Once the audience is convinced it is nothing but an ordinary dough used to make puries, the magician's eyes would be covered with it. Then his assistants would put one blindfold upon other, and finally, his head will be wrapped in a black sack. With this solid covering on, Sorcar would invite volunteers from the audience onto the stage and ask them to write out questions or arithmetic problems on a blackboard: like additions or multiplications. Sorcar would answer the questions and do the sums. As people began to think assistants were passing on the answers to the magician through a sophisticated code, Sorcar would ask volunteers to draw anything, but leave it incomplete. For example, half a fish. Instantaneously, he would complete the picture, with the lines extended perfectly! I write this memoir in a time when lots of people cannot see barefaced lies peddled by men in power. I cannot but think they are the exact opposites of the magician who could see through his blindfolds.

Finally, on the bare stage of the New Empire theatre—we could see the wall behind—the magician made a red Impala convertible filled with half-a-dozen young women smiling and frantically waving at you vanish in a trice. (Another time, it was a live elephant on stage!) Then, he would himself disappear from the stage and materialise in the last row on the balcony in a moment.

* * *

In 1957, Prime Minister Jawaharlal Nehru inaugurated the Electrical Multiple Unit (EMU) train, popularly known as the electric train, at Howrah. In the Eastern Railway, the first section that was blessed with this high-tech wonder was the Howrah-Bandel section. The EMUs were (Can you believe it?) trains without engines! That, plus the sliding doors, big windows, brightly painted green and beige exterior, and no toilets, were no less magical than Magician Sorcar. As those trains didn't have stairs leading from the ground level to the coaches, they would stop only at stations with high platforms. And unlike steam locos, EMUs would pick up speed within seconds and zoom out of the platforms with terrorised passengers within and awestruck onlookers outside.

On Sunday afternoons, Baba would often take Ruby and me for short excursions on electric trains. (I don't know why mom never accompanied us on those trips.) When EMUs started running beyond Bandel, a couple of Sundays we visited some relatives, unannounced, at a place called Pandua. We walked out of the quiet station and walked into an even quieter small town that was still having its afternoon siesta.

One of the boys in the family, Golap, slightly older than me, played the tabla brilliantly. As his nimble fingers danced on the tabla, they created almost tactile acoustic patterns. I used to watch Golap in utter disbelief and marvel how anyone could do such a goddamned thing. (My wonder for musicians hasn't gone down one jot. Even now I am amazed when someone plays a musical instrument beautifully, or sings with every note in place. How do they do it?)

I am sure no other relations of ours lived where an EMU train could take us, because we didn't visit another home during these expeditions. But we did make a number of trips to nowhere. They used to be journeys in sparsely filled trains that would be unimaginable these days. As air blasted in through windows and brushed our faces, we would go past the suburbia into a green country and watch women tending babies, children pushing tyre-less bicycle wheels with a stick, and dogs sleeping contentedly. We would get off at any station that caught Baba's fancy and walk down to a roadside eatery to eat rasgullas. Baba said it was always safe to eat rasgullas outside: they couldn't be made with stale cottage cheese. He ought to have known. One of his many had-been businesses was an eatery.

The world is full of wonders that cost nothing.

29| Visitors from Everywhere

Many years later, as he faced the firing squad,
Colonel Aureliano Buendía was to remember that distant afternoon
when his father took him to discover ice.
— Gabriel García Márquez, *One Hundred Years of Solitude*

Like Marquez's lovable colonel, I too was taken by Father to discover ice in an autumn evening. An American troupe of ice-skaters had come to town to perform a show named *Holiday on Ice.* As red, purple, yellow, and blue beams of conical lights reflected from the mirror-like floor (the word disco hadn't been invented), young men and women skaters in gorgeous costumes wove brilliant patterns on a temporary ice rink, with equally colourful sashes flying from their arms and waistbands. It was a brief journey to another world. For the month or so while the troupe was in town and a few months thereafter, people of Calcutta discussed nothing else. Some fortunate girls would later be blessed with Holiday-on-Ice frocks!

My sister was. I do not know if my friend Bhawani, who too lived in Calcutta as a child, had a Holiday-on-Ice frock because we met as adults. After reading this story on my blog, she reminded me of another fascinating show. It was called Circerama, but I am not sure how it was spelt. It was a circular theatre which had no chairs. The audience stood in the middle and watched images projected on multiple screens all around. The 360° images had been captured by multiple cameras. Being there, we felt we were travelling on a bus in New York, with the Hudson, the East River, and the Empire State Building moving behind. This would be old hat for the present Google generation, but back in the 1960s, it was a marvel beyond compare. Much later, as I drove under the Hudson through the Holland Tunnel with its white tiled walls, it was déjà vu.

Other afternoon adventures that were big deals were watching Davis Cup tennis matches from the make-shift galleries in South Club. (Sadly, Ruby, and needless to say Mother, were excluded from this.) Roy Emerson, John Newcomb, and Fred Stolle were all familiar names in Tennis for a child who read the sports page of *The Statesman* every day. And I was fortunate to see some of those great men play in Calcutta. But the match that I would never forget happened between ….

Before I complete the story, one afternoon, as we were going through the turnstile at the South Club, Baba said to me in Bangla in a normal voice, 'Don't turn around, but see who is behind us.'

But I did turn around and a shiver ran through my spine. A dark athletic young man was behind us: Ramanathan Krishnan.

The greatest Indian tennis player, who had played two Wimbledon semi-finals, was in white tennis clothes, carrying a heavy bag. I was dying to tell him, 'Sir, best wishes for your match.' But my tongue betrayed me, the fool tied itself into a knot. It was a Davis Cup match and Krishnan was to play the second singles of the day and the fifth match in the rubber. Memory of the first singles of the day has been erased from my memory, but at the end of it, the rubber was tied at 2-2. It was the finals, the winner would go on to meet the previous year's champions, Australia in what was called the Challenge Round. India had never been in the Challenge round before.

In that best-of-five-sets tie, Ramanathan Krishnan would play Tomas Koch, the Brazilian National Champion. Koch, a lefthander, was a brilliant player who some tennis analysts believed would become another Rod Lever.

Koch led Krishnan 2 sets to 1, 5 games to 2 in the fourth set when play was stopped because of bad light. (Was it to give an unfair advantage to a tiring Krishnan? I don't know. But the Brazilians were good sports, they didn't complain. Or more likely, Koch was confident of victory the following day.)

The next morning, although the result was almost a foregone conclusion, the stands were full. Calcuttans, a sturdy lot, didn't lose hope easily!) Krishnan was trailing—if my memory serves me right, 0-30 (2 games to 5, 1 set to 2)—when Koch played a beautiful passing shot. Krishnan looked on passively; making no attempt to return the ball as a collective sigh went up in the gallery. Why the hell didn't he dive?

Another point would eliminate India from Davis Cup.

And then, Ramanathan Krishnan scripted one of the most memorable come-backs in the history of world tennis. From 0-40, he saved at least three match points and went on to win the game. After that, Krishnan was at his sublime best. He passed Koch time and again with delectable passing shots that barely crossed the net and kissed the lines. Krishnan won the set 7-5, and went on to win the match and the rubber.

These days, when heads of states visit India, they usually give Kolkata a miss. Sometime in the year 2000, when Bill Clinton visited India, in a public toilet in Hazra Park, beside a handbill stuck on the wall promising cheap and hassle-free abortion, I saw a small hand-written poster: "Bill Clinton, GO BACK!" I wondered why whoever stuck the poster chose that particular place. There was no chance that the American president would pass water anywhere nearby. He wouldn't even visit the city. Contrastingly, in our childhood, every visiting dignitary would visit Calcutta. Nikita Khrushchev came. So did Zhou Enlai and Dalai Lama. People would discuss the visits excitedly.

An event that left a deep impression on my young mind was Yuri Gagarin's voyage to space when I was 10. The next day's newspapers brought the news. I would have missed the school bus that morning. Motilalda took me to school. As we walked the two miles, we discussed what exactly was meant by going to space and how it happened. I am sure that we discussed some hypotheses that would not come to the head of any space scientist. Incidentally, Gagarin too visited the city towards the end of the year.

Valentina Tereshkova, who piloted a spaceship for three days in June 1963 too came to the city. Her visit was an inspiring moment, partly because of her gender and partly because hers was a journey from a textile factory to space. (She had been a factory worker before being chosen to be the first woman astronaut.) Students of many girls' schools lined up the streets of Calcutta to greet her.

Continuing with visits by dignitaries, the biggest event was when Queen Elizabeth II visited January 1961. A big crowd had gathered on the terrace of my Pishemoshai's office in Ganesh Chandra Avenue to see her. It was a three-storey building. Below, the footpaths were packed with eager onlookers. HRH The Queen, then in her mid-thirties, looked exquisitely beautiful in a pink dress. She stood in a roofless convertible saloon, waving, as the car moved along, slowly. The bald-headed prince consort in funereal black stood beside her and waved too, but no one cared for him.

Pishemoshai had a penchant for doing the unusual. As refreshment for the guests who had gathered on his office terrace, he provided fiery hot chānāchuṛ in a jumbo paper cone. I could watch the queen only through my tears. There were "oohs" and "aahs" all around.

30|The Company I Kept

When we were children, parents spent little time for their offspring.

Can I make such a sweeping statement? I think I can. Parents in our childhood certainly were far more relaxed about the future of their children than the parents today are about theirs. Most of my friends, I am inclined to believe, grew up without close parental supervision. In their free time, kids were left to their own devices. The rat race hadn't begun. A friend of mine later summed up the scenario neatly: 'We grew up like weeds.'

I too grew up like weeds more or less, but in my case, the situation was different from my friends because I had the company of people who assisted my dad in his business. I have already written about my childhood mentors Rajenda and Motilalda. Let me tell you some untold stories about them and introduce a few more.

Motilalda, a tall, bony man who could be anywhere between 30 and 60 was a vegetable vendor in the morning and dad's handyman for the rest of the day. He read newspapers, wrote in a neat hand, bought our provisions, maintained accounts, and fudged them. Motilalda enlightened me on many things, from Yuri Gagarin's journey to space, to how people lived in villages, to how biscuits were made.

He used to be in white usually, but otherwise, he was a colourful personality. Although he lived alone in a tiny one-room cottage (there still were authentic cottages in Calcutta), he often talked about his other house in the village, which happened to be two storeyed and big. He also spoke about the fish in his pond, his fields of golden paddy, and the glorious cows that produced tankers of milk. Besides, he was on intimate terms with a few leading film stars. With the benefit of hindsight, I would say he never told a lie. Rather, he lived in two worlds. And who can say that the world that can be touched and seen is the only world?

* * *

A carpenter by name Mukundo was a regular visitor to our house. Father was fond of tinkering with whatever furniture we had. Sundays, consequently, would often come alive on our terrace with the sound of sawing and hammering. What had been a cot earlier turned into a partition thanks to Mukundo's expertise. A few years later, the same piece of furniture might have outlived its utility and be reborn as a bookshelf. When we were children, three R's meant Reading, Writing, and Arithmetic. In the hugely wasteful world today, children are taught in school three new R's: Reduce, Reuse, Recycle. Fifty years ago, the concept was not taught at school, it was a fact of life.

While Mukundoda worked, I was fascinated to watch sweat dripping from the deep furrows on his brow. He became the work he was doing. Much later, one evening as I watched Ali Akbar Khan playing the sarod immersed in his music, Mukundoda's image flashed before my eyes.

I would often volunteer to help him by holding the piece of wood he was working on. Over time, Mukundoda took me as an apprentice and would allow me to first scrape wood with sandpaper and later to use the plane to smoothen a surface, or put together a dove-tail joint with wooden pegs, and so on. Later, when I had to learn carpentry in high school, I found the tasks easy.

But more than teaching me how to use a chisel or a saw, he inspired in me a deep and irrevocable respect for manual labour. An African American leader, Booker T. Washington said: "No race can prosper till it learns there is as much dignity in tilling a field as in writing a poem." In America, people who work standing up are not considered inferior to those who earn sitting down. Later, I have seen that in the USA, a plumber who repairs the gutter of your house speaks with the same assurance as the architect who designed the building. Washington was right: if India hasn't prospered as much as it could have, one of the reasons is that men like Mukundoda are nailed close to the bottom of the social ladder.

There were other interesting visitors to our house. Bolaida, a fishmonger in the local bazaar, would maintain accounts in a small notebook even as he cleaned, cut, weighed, and packed pieces of fish in dry leaves. Fish, like many other things, would be bought on credit. Bolaida visited us once a month to collect his dues. The man who people saw in a lungi and a singlet through the month would transform himself by wearing a fine shirt and a crisp dhoti during his client visits. He sat opposite Baba at his desk, had tea, and discussed politics. He would break into a loud guffaw now and then.

Let me complete my memories of the ordinary but special working-class Indians I met as a child by returning to Rajenda. Rajenda and his wife, Sudhadi lived near our house in a ten feet by ten feet room with a solitary window looking out to a crowded road where girls played hopscotch and women collected water from a standpipe.

In our house, Rajenda wasn't hard-pressed for time. Often, he used to read. He would also read aloud—in his deep voice—poems of Rabindranath:

> My mind, wake up for the great pilgrimage
> In India, on the shore of the ocean of many a sage.

Apart from his love for poetry, Rajenda had enormous practical sense. Once, when I was slightly older, I hurt my foot while playing football, which used to be a barefoot affair. The last three toes of my right foot were pointing at a different direction and I couldn't wear shoes. The injury was not considered serious enough to be reported to elders, let alone a doctor. Rajenda massaged my foot for weeks with hot mustard oil until the toes returned to their rightful place. Neither the patient nor the physiotherapist knew how serious an issue dislocation of a bone might be. Or perhaps, the therapist knew, but didn't mention it in order not to frighten his child patient.

31| The Fire that Wasn't

I love New York, even though it isn't mine, the way something has to be, a tree or a street or a house, something, anyway, that belongs to me because I belong to it.[xxv]
- Truman Capote

Like Truman Capote, I too believe my city Kolkata belongs to me because I belong to her. When she was known as Calcutta, we lived in a house overlooking an arterial road of the city, as I've told you. On our side of the road towards the south, there was a tram-and-bus-stop some 50 metres away. Between the bus stop and our house, there was what we Indians call a petrol bunk or petrol pump. A native speaker of English will refer to it as a filling station or petrol station. In a corner of the petrol bunk, there was a hydraulic lift on which cars and trucks would be raised and their undercarriage washed with water jets that made a loud hissing sound.

My study had a window overlooking the petrol pump. I would often sit there and watch the city flowing like a mighty river below. One evening, when the sun had just set, a petrol tanker stood in the forecourt as petrol was being unloaded from it into an underground reservoir through a fat rubber pipe. It was just another usual day, lots of people were waiting at the bus stop and there were many more on footpaths.

Suddenly, I observed a curious thing happening. Petrol was overflowing the underground storage tank. It started innocuously, like many disasters do, with no one noticing. But in a short while, lovely little rivulets of petrol started flowing in different directions from the point where the rubber pipe was connected to the valve on the top of the underground tank. Soon, a crowd of curious onlookers gathered, talking and gesticulating. Apparently, the tanker operator had left his post and gone for chai, and others were too excited and confused to turn off the connection, as it often happens when people come across a serious danger. By the time someone regained his presence of mind and turned the tap off, the forecourt of the filling station was flooded with petrol. Apparently oblivious of the lurking threat, the crowd loved the excitement, and were busy discussing possible and impossible remedies.

From my second-floor window, I saw all this and then, noticed a new onlooker casually approaching the trouble-spot to get a closer look. He was one among a hundred people maybe, but there was a serious issue. This fellow had a lighted cigarette in hand! No one noticed him as he approached from behind. The amber liquid continued to dance its deathly dance.

Then someone screamed. The bystanders yelled at the man and pounced upon him. He too realized his folly just in time and threw the lighted cigarette as far away as he could … but unfortunately, in a wrong direction!

It flew in a perfect parabola towards disaster and the next morning's headlines, and landed inches short of a stream of petrol. For a few moments, the world, including the life of yours truly, hung by a slender thread. I was a child then, but was old enough to know that a fire in a big petrol tank would blow up everything around, every onlooker, including me. But the spectacle held me in its thrall, I couldn't turn away and run, just as the crowd couldn't.

Fortunately, a smart young man trod on the burning cigarette to save maybe, a hundred lives. Maybe, this memoir should have been dedicated to the unknown hero and saviour who received no award for bravery and quick thinking.

Three fire engines arrived within minutes; a fire station was less than half a mile from our house. The firemen cordoned off the area, put a barrier of sand around the pool, pushed away the tanker physically (the trained firefighters naturally had the sense not to turn on the ignition of the vehicle!). They also got electricity switched off in the area. All this happened within maybe, ten minutes.

As the sudden power-cut forced a crowd of confused talkative people out of the cinema into an unreal darkness, the spilled petrol dried off peacefully.

I have thought about this incident multiple times. I think there is indeed something called destiny in our life. That you are reading the story, dear Reader, was a part of your destiny.

32| Writers at a Post Office

After living a glorious life spanning 163 years, Mr Telegram died in India on 15 July 2013, when emails and text messages made living pointless for him. The first telegram in India had been sent in 1850 from Calcutta to Diamond Harbour, 50 kilometres away. Two years later, the first Indian adhesive postage stamp was issued.

And a hundred years after that, collecting stamps was a favourite pastime for a lot of Indian boys. (Curiously, like flying kites and football, this hobby too was gender specific. There wasn't a girl stamp collector that I know of.)

Besides offering a sense of possession and pride, the hobby also opened up a window to the world. Normally, I would have nothing to do with Dominica, or St. Lucia, or say, Hungary, but tiny pieces of papers from these faraway lands found a cosy home in my stamp album and created for me a bond with them. While I was in school, I got myself a beautiful custom-made stamp album with black Rexine-bound hard covers that held together a fat sheaf of papers with copper nuts-and-bolts along its left edge. The thick pages had tiny squares printed in fine blue lines. Used stamps were removed from envelopes by soaking them in water and fixed on these pages with delicate paper hinges. We often exchanged stamps with fellow collectors. And that is how we began trade talks at a tender age.

If stamps were important to children, letters played a weighty role in the life of adults. The postal department was absurdly reliable. If you sent a letter from any corner of the country, say Kanya Kumari, it would invariably reach the addressee, whether in Calcutta, Karimgunj, or Kohima within three to five working days. A postman in smart khaki uniform would climb up two floors to deliver letters twice every day. Most of them were for Mother.

The letters Ma wrote (and the many that she received) would contain mundane details of everyday life, like who had come home, or what had happened at a school function, not to mention weather bulletins. A confession about stealing potassium cyanide on a postcard was a rare occurrence. These days, people exchange such information over the mobile phone and spend enormous lengths of time on the tiny instrument! Those days, the local post office was as important as the mobile phone is today.

I was in primary school when I became my family's designated functionary for everything relating to postal services. I would often go to the Kalighat post office, which buzzed with activity. Post-office clerks used to be extremely hard-working and bad-tempered. Besides dropping letters in big letterboxes, buying stamps and postal stationery after standing in a long queue, sending occasional money orders and telegrams (even longer queues), I paid some minor taxes there. One had to pay a small annual licence fee for a radio receiver back in the 1950s. As late as in 1984 I paid the annual tax on my scooter at a post office.

Outside, Kalighat post office, a few manifestly malnourished men with sunken cheeks sat on rickety armless wooden chairs with small, equally malnourished desks in front. They were the "writers", who would pen a letter for you or fill in your money-order form, in case you couldn't read and write English. (Long after the Brits left our shores, Indians continued to use English to fill in cheques and money order forms, and to call their dogs. (Those days,, pet dogs usually had English names like Tommy, Jimmy or Millie.)

Once, an evidently poor man requested me to fill in a money order form. I agreed because I thought I ought to help him save a few annas which a writer would charge.

Looking back, I am not sure who was more badly off, the man who approached me, or the man who I denied a legitimate income.

33| A Wake-up Call

Compared to the post office, the United Bank of India a few blocks away from our home in the big building called Amulya Mansion was a far more relaxed place. Few visited banks those days; most people didn't have bank accounts. Salaries were paid in cash and were mostly spent by the month-end. My mother had a savings account with hardly any savings in it. Father too never saved nothing, but he had to have a current account for his business.

Over time, an employee of the street-corner bank, Chitta Babu, became a friend of my parents. Every year in April or May, when mother corrected a few hundred scripts of secondary exams, Chitta Babu would come home on a Sunday morning and add up all the scores in a trice like a magician, and join us for lunch. That was professional expertise. Do you remember how Charlie Chaplin counted currency notes as a bank cashier in Monsieur Verdoux?

I too could have helped my mom in adding up the scores, but she perhaps thought it would be morally wrong to get such serious work done by a child. I don't think my parents paid Chitta Babu for his services. In India, lots of transactions are carried out in the currency of friendship. And maybe, it was truer then.

Banks were quite seriously fortified those days. A four feet high, solid wooden partition separated the front of the banking hall from the rest of it. Above the partition, a heavy wire mesh screen went right up to the ceiling. Customers were confined to the front portion, while the bank staff sat in their big cage, within which there were smaller cages for individual cashiers. If an outsider had to enter the area reserved for employees, they could do so only after obtaining permission. Within the cage, a long desk ran along the length of the partition at which clerks sat. Cheques, tokens, and cash used to change hands through small holes on the wire mesh. The first teller hadn't been born yet.

One day, dad sent me to cash a cheque, which wasn't an unfamiliar errand for me. Usually, I would deposit a cheque and collect a metal token in the morning and go back leisurely in the afternoon to exchange the token for cash. Life moved at a gentle pace.

I guess I was barely over four feet then, because I could just about see through the wire mesh above the partition. I could see what was happening away from the partition, but couldn't see the desk right below, where the counter clerk sat; I could only see his head. On that particular day, I reached the bank at around half ten. Although the office was scheduled to open at 10, I saw no head at the "Current Accounts" counter. There were not many customers either. I waited for the clerk to arrive.

Quite some time passed, no one came. Transactions started to pick up at other counters; many customers came and left, but there was none at the Current Account counter to accept my cheque. At length, I peeped through the wire mesh and tried to attract the attention of a man who was at a table a little away. But the middle-aged man in thick glasses was too preoccupied to notice a small boy fidgeting on the other side of the wire mesh. So, I stood on my toes and looked around to talk to someone else. And what do I see?

Right below my nose, the clerk manning the counter is fast asleep, resting his peaceful head on the desk.

34| Street Cries

My childhood home was anchored on a sea of unmelodious sounds. Waves of noise splashed upon us all the time. On the main road beside our home, trams and buses would run almost until midnight, with their associated din. At times, a vehicle would screech to a halt, or an impatient driver would keep honking. In the petrol station beside our house, the hydraulic jack that lifted vehicles would produce a shrill ear-splitting sibilant sound from time to time. These incidents would produce frequent spikes in the otherwise steady graph of noise. Nights were not quiet either. Our house was not far from a major crematorium, and every night, pallbearers would carry a corpse or two on a flimsy cot, all the while calling a god named Hari above as loudly as they could, possibly to ward off evil spirits. You might think that accompanying a person along his last journey should be a sombre affair, but my community thinks otherwise.

The morning was ushered in not by the Sun God, but by the clang of the first tramcar rolling out unfailingly at 4 AM. The fizzy sound of roads being washed by water jets would follow soon. Beside the portico of Amulya Mansion, trucks covered with tarpaulins would unload newspapers.

I must add that we happily slept through all the commotion. We were aware of these nocturnal issues, but only theoretically. However, our guests just couldn't sleep in our house. Those who slept doggedly and survived the first tram had to wake up soon: newspaper vendors would fight noisily to get their quota of papers even before crows began to caw.

Newspapers weren't in short supply. The vendors fought possibly because they didn't have the patience, time, or discipline to stand in a queue. They would surround a newspaper truck from all sides and each one of them would try to snatch their quota asap, yelling as loudly as they could. In the process, everyone got delayed.

Later in the day, in front of the cinema opposite our house, vendors hawked a variety of small eats during intervals in movies, screaming the quality and price of their wares. Not a word of what they said could be followed, but the place came alive three times a day, seven days a week. Besides small eats, a popular product those days were shabbily printed booklets giving the lyrics of the songs and an incomplete storyline of the film that was being shown on the day. The story would build up some kind of suspense and always end with the sentence: Watch the rest on the silver screen.

The tinkle of the bell in the rickshaw puller's hand had a quaint musical charm. And lazy afternoons and Sunday mornings would come alive with lovely street cries.

I cannot recall a Sunday morning in my childhood without two things: the waft of mutton being cooked and the trader of old newspapers going around with a gunny sack on his back calling out: *'Khabarer k-a-a-g-o-o-o-j!'* The men were invariably thin, with their ribs showing through the torn undershirt they wore. They usually cheated their clients while weighing the papers, but despite all their efforts, they were invariably very poor, perhaps just a shade better than the multitude of beggars on the city's streets. Often, these traders couldn't pay for the papers they bought. They would leave their weighing balance and weights as security, go away, and come back to pay after selling their stock-in-trade to scrap dealers.

In my childhood, there was also a popular barter system in which vendors, mostly women, handed over utensils in exchange for old clothes. Afternoons were their preferred business hours. They would announce their arrival with lovely singsong calls. The barter system survives to this day, but one doesn't hear them calling out. Besides, there were men offering a range of services like duplicating keys, chipping grinding stones, sharpening knives, and engraving names on utensils.

Each of these tradesmen had their characteristic ways of attracting customers, mostly through singsong street cries. But the key maker needed no verbal effort: he would clank dozens of keys on a large ring to announce his arrival. Another silent tradesman, seen only during winters, would pronounce his presence with the twang of a string instrument, his carding bow.

Back in my childhood, all mattresses and quilts were made of natural cotton, which became hard and lumpy every few years. The men, who we called dhunuris, would unstitch a quilt (or mattress), take the cotton out, and run their bowstring repeatedly through the sticky mass of cotton. The process, known as carding, would loosen the cotton and make it fluffy. (Wikipedia tells me that the carding bow was invented in India in the second century CE.) As the fleecy cotton captured more air in their fibres, quilts became warmer too. Snuggling under a soft, newly remade quilt in a winter's night was one of the finest pleasures that childhood offered us.

The men who roughened grinding stones with a chisel shouted '*Sheeel katta-a-ai.*' Neither the words nor the tune ever varied. The engravers sang out: *'Bā- ā-sōne nāām lekh-ā-ā-ā-be-e-e-e-n'*. *(Wr-i-i-i-te your n-a-a-a-mes on pots and pans!)* Their voice would trail off slowly, to accentuate the loneliness of the afternoon. Obviously, they eked out a modest living by writing the owners' names on steel, aluminium, and brass vessels, and fortunately for them, no one ever thought of what earthly purpose it served.

Another vendor was a man who carried a black steel trunk on his head. For some reason, he never advertised his products, at least not verbally. He was the only silent vendor on the streets of Calcutta. He would put down his trunk and take out yellow, orange, and pink pastries. One of the few regrets I have in life is that I never got a chance to taste his tantalising pastries and cakes.

Finally, the vendors I remember most vividly would always be in a sparkling white shirt and a short dhoti. They carried earthen pots of indigenous ice cream on their heads and called out *'Mālā-ā-ā-i barō-ō-ō-ō-f'* in a calm, unhurried voice. A particular man among them was punctilious about time; he would pass by exactly at midnight. I never saw him as I was tucked in well before that hour; but whenever I woke up in a dark night hearing his mysterious voice, I would also hear the wall clock gong twelve times before I drifted off to sleep again. In my somnolence, I imagined a slender old man in white dhoti and shirt trudging along, carrying an earthen pot of kulfi mālāi on his head. I often wondered who would buy kulfi at that hour, particularly in cold wintry nights.

One day, I asked my friend Ravi, a Tamil by birth and a Bengali by circumstances, about the mysterious midnight kulfi mālāi seller, 'I've never seen him, have you?'

'No. How can I? Don't you know? He's heard, but never seen.'

'Why?'

'How can you see him? He's only a spirit, a ghost!'

Looking back through a field glass of fifty years, I think maybe, Ravi was right. Perhaps the old man was actually not human. Perhaps he was a visitor from the netherworld, who reminded humans of the long icy night that awaits every one of them.

35| Printed Letters

That morning, I was reading "Water drips, leaves tremble."
To me, it was the first poem written by the original poet. ...
Water kept dripping and leaves kept trembling
in my consciousness through the day.
– Rabindranath Tagore in his memoir *Jeevansmriti*

I was introduced to the world of printed letters through a book that told the story of the Ramayana in comic strips. The first book we read perhaps remains with us for ever. I can recall the colour of the cover page (grey) and the size of the book (large, children's, portrait orientation, possibly 7"x10").

Those days, an average middle-class Bengali child began reading with short stories by Upendra Kishore Ray Chowdhury. Later, they would read Abanindranath Tagore and Sukumar Ray.

Dakshinaranjan Mitra Majumdar's *Thakurmar Jhuli (Grandma's Sack)* and a few other books with similarly eponymous titles were collections of fairy tales that smelt of the earth and the waters of Bengal. Generations of Bengali children read those books, until a gust of "English-medium education"—long after the Brits left—changed their language, and to an extent, cultural moorings. Oral history tells us that *Thakurmar Jhuli* was originally told by a village drummer or dhuli.

> Sōnā Dhuli sat under a peepul tree and told tales to his bemused audience. He became famous, but as he stopped drumming in order to tell stories, he also became poorer. It happens if you leave a secure career in search of the esoteric. Sōnā Dhuli didn't have enough to eat, but remained a storyteller till the end. Dakshinaranjan heard the stories during his visits to Dighpāit, his mother's village.[xxvi]

Dakshinaranjan did a great service to Bangla literature by retrieving the tales from a remote village in the district of Mymansingh in East Bengal. Many more similar gems would have been lost when literature was passed on through speech.

* * *

I was fortunate to have reached this world before the television did. Primary schools were much more relaxed places those days; mine used to be over by 10:30 in the morning, as I've said. I returned to an empty home as my sister Ruby studied at a day school and Mother too would be in hers.

I spent the afternoons alone. As languid street cries of men offering a variety of services wafted in from the deserted streets and crows cawed to accentuate the loneliness, I spent hours watching—incidentally, like the physicist Richard Feynman—ants undertaking trans-continental journeys in the cracks of the parapet wall on our terrace. But I reached very wrong conclusions, which led me to an act for which I have always been ashamed. (This is what I promised to confess in the beginning of this memoir.)

On our terrace, there were red ants and black ants. Red ants would bite at times, although they were hardly painful. But their tinier, black cousins were peace-loving creatures; they wouldn't sting. Unlike humans, the two distinct tribes never fought. Each moved in long rows, but their paths wouldn't cross.

One afternoon, when a red ant bit me, it got into my head that they had to be eliminated. I killed every red ant I saw that afternoon, hundreds of them. It was a brutal ethnic cleansing. I will die carrying the shame of that daylight massacre. … This is what unchecked power can do even to timid child.

* * *

Later, when I grew up a little, my dog Toffee taught me what unconditional love was long before I got to hear the expression.

Besides spending time with ants and my pet, I would also read storybooks, mostly lying prone on a mat with a pillow under my chest. We had a fairly large collection of children's fiction. More importantly, Ma introduced me to the treasure trove that her school library was; in the evening, I would invariably check her bag to see what books she had bought for me.

Bangla translations of Dickens, Jules Verne, Robert Louis Stevenson, and Alexander Dumas were my staple. I read *The Treasure Island* and every novel of Jules Verne many times over. Captain Nemo was my childhood hero, more so because he was an Indian prince who ruled the depths of the oceans. And of course *The Treasure Island.* I'd often imagine an old sailor climbing up our stairs … the wooden stump that served as one of his legs making an eerie noise …

> Fifteen men on a dead man's chest,
> Yo-ho-ho and a bottle of rum …
> And the devil will do the rest.

Another book I'd go back to again and again was Bibhuti Bhushan's *Chānder Pāhāṛ (The Mountain of the Moon).* Abanindranath Tagore, a legendary painter, also wrote, rather, painted stories for children. Rare was a Bengali child who didn't read his *Nālak, Rāj Kāhini*, and *Shakuntala.* Among the other must-read books was Sukumar Ray's *Ābōl Tābōl (Gobbledygook)*, a collection of nonsense verses which remains unmatched to this day in the two languages that I know, even after considering Edward Leer and Ogden Nash. And of course, Sukumar Ray's prose: *Ha ja ba ra la (Topsy-turvy Tale)* and *Pāglā Dāshu (Dāshu is Nuts).* Sukumar Ray was Upendrakishore's son. As children, we knew Sukumar Ray's son, Satyajit Ray only as a filmmaker. Later, Satyajit would pick up the pen and create the legendary private detective Feluda and the scientific genius Professor Shanku for children and adults. Children's literature in Bangla would have been much poorer but for these three generations of Rays.

I subscribed to the children's magazine *Rāmdhanu, (The Rainbow).* It was a matter of pride to find the slim periodical in our letter box with my name printed on the sleeve. The magazine was edited by Kshitindra Narayan Bhattacharya, who wrote science fiction for children. (For his day job, he taught chemistry at a college.) The magazine-office-cum-printing press-cum-the editor's-residence was near our home, in Townsend Road, although the place was no longer at the town's end then. Kshitindra Narayan was the first author I met in flesh and blood; I was nervous. But he put me at ease in minutes and talked as if he was talking to an equal.

Besides, there was another magazine, *Suktara (The Evening Star)* that our newspaper supplier, Master Moshai delivered. In *Suktara*, almost every month, there used to be a mushy story about an orphan boy, badly treated by stepmothers or masters, run away and return years later after he made it big.

My friend Ashish Sarbagya ran away from home when we were in the Class IX. Afflicted by polio when he was little, Ashish walked with a limp. He lived near my house and we would often walk together to school. He walked fast and was none the worse for his physical challenge. I don't know if Ashish has made it big. Nobody has heard of him since that day.

36| A Bit of Violence

A watched pot doesn't boil. The shadow of the portico of the petrol station beside our house would take an eternity to reach a keenly watched imaginary line to announce it was 4 PM. I had to wait for that magic moment to start off for Kalighat Park, which I have described in some detail in *The Plural City*. My faithful furry four-legged companion, Toffee too would be eagerly waiting for the afternoon of fun and frolic. In the park, I would tie him to a post and play cricket or football. Toffee was a cheerful fellow. He would watch us play and wag his tail vigorously whenever I went close to him while playing. He loved the outing and shook hands with whoever would care to.

* * *

Memory is a sieve. We do not realise when unpleasant experiences trickle through it and vanish. If, after reading this memoir so far, you think everything was lovely in the city of Calcutta in the 1950s and '60s, it wouldn't be my fault. That's how memory works.

Unlike some Indian communities like Marathas, Jats, or Tamils, Bengalis are not considered soldierly. But they are not unfond of violence. In the city of my childhood, older boys of a pārā would often wage war against boys from another pārā. When forces were evenly matched on two sides, the preferred weapon was soda-water bottles, which would explode on strong impacts and if directed accurately, cause grievous injury. But more often, the warriors would look for an opportunity to capture a lone soldier from the enemy camp and beat the poor fellow to pulp. I witnessed such cowardly violence a couple of times. It has had two effects on my psyche. First, I don't think I will ever be able to hurt a defenceless person. Second, I've always had a mortal fear of physical violence.

Later, when we would be in college, a collective madness would grip West Bengal, resulting in violent death of thousands of young people. The 1960s was also a time when possibly the most asymmetric war in history reached a climax in Vietnam, which ended in the comprehensive defeat of the much bigger of the two adversaries. With that conflict playing out on the world scene, in West Bengal, a militant political agitation began: the Naxalite movement. The agitation and its participants acquired their name from a peasant uprising in a remote hamlet in Naxalbari in North Bengal, which began when 11 people, including nine women and a baby strapped to her mother died in police firing on 25 May 1967.

While the rebellion in Naxalbari originated as peasants' struggle against exploitation by landlords, the Naxalite movement that followed was very different from the original uprising. The Naxalite rebels, who were mostly students and young people from cities and small towns, didn't focus on mass movements by peasants. Instead, they tried to begin an armed revolution to destroy the Indian state and replace it with a more equitable one. However, soon, the undertaking drifted into almost random killing of people who Naxalites considered "class enemies". The state retaliated with even more violence.

No one knows how many young men (and women) got killed in that sad chapter of our lifetime. For boys of my generation in West Bengal, being alive depended on the political path they chose, and to an extent, chance. My friends and I lived our early youth in the fear of becoming undeserving targets of violence.

No memoir written by someone of my generation from West Bengal can be complete without references to the Naxalbari uprising. I will get back to it later in this chronicle. But for now, it's time for happier memories.

37| Fun and Frolic

The Calcutta Football League played an important part in the lives of young men and boys. The league had four divisions, but except for the first, others didn't matter. Every one of us—by default—was a supporter of one of the three major teams: East Bengal, Mohan Bagan, or Mohammedan Sporting.

Sporting clubs had their designated grounds in the Maidan, a thousand-acre green tract between Chowringhee Road and the River Hooghly. As no permanent structure is allowed there, the clubs had tents in the Maidan, which were often large and elaborate. Only the three big clubs I've named had galleries (rows of sloping wooden benches on three sides of their football grounds. On the fourth side was the rampart, that is, an open space separated from the pitch by a strong wire mesh and barbed wire. Eager spectators who couldn't buy or afford to buy tickets would jostle and fight in the ramparts to get glimpses of a match, at times, with rudimentary periscopes! The ramparts were the equivalent of the amplifiers fitted outside music concerts for the hoi polloi. The system accepted that those who couldn't afford to pay too had the right to entertainment.

The three-sided wooden enclosures were apologies of stadiums, but the excitement around football was authentic. Victory of one's team in a derby would lead to excitement and bragging rights for some in schools and offices, and dejection for others. Football hooliganism was common. Dissatisfied supporters of a losing team pelted stones at the peaceful store-windows and glow signs. There was a time when all the glow signs in the central districts of Calcutta were covered by wire mesh.

However, despite the passion around football, the glamour sport was cricket, the excitement about which was restricted to a solitary annual international test match played in Eden Gardens, which genteel people went to watch carrying oranges and sandwiches.

The Ranji Stadium in Eden Gardens, named after the Sir Ranjitsinhji, an Indian princeling who had played for the English cricket team, looked more like a stadium compared to the football galleries, although it was nothing compared to the imposing brick-and-mortar structure that stands there today. The enduring memories of a test match etched in my mind are a helmet-less Pankaj Roy or Nari Contractor ducking away from Alan Davidson bouncers in an ethereal Garden of Eden.

The cricket spectators of Calcutta were serious, knowledgeable, and almost entirely male. Once, there was a controversy about the Australian left-arm fast bowler Ian Meckiff's bowling action. Meckiff played 18 test matches between 1957 and 63. Indian umpires wouldn't call him. During a test match in Calcutta while Meckiff was bowling, a spectator shouted from the stands—and the rest of the crowd heard him in total silence, 'Mr Meckiff! Next summer, English umpires will tell you that you chuck. A chucker is a chucker is a chucker!' (I wasn't at the stadium, the incident is a part of Kolkata's sporting folklore.)

Fortunately for Mr Meckiff, he was left out of the Australian squad to England in 1961. But two years later, an Australian umpire no-balled him four times in his first over in South Africa, and that was the end of his cricketing career.

Not many actually saw Contractor, Davidson, or Sobers in flesh and blood. (I was fortunate because my Gandhian dad was crazy about cricket and tennis.) The rest of the country had to make do with the running commentary given by Pearson Surita, Berry Sarbadhikari, and Vizzy in English and Kamal Bhattacharya, Pushpen Sarkar and Ajay Bose in Bangla, who were local icons. They added to the five days of a test match an aura that was perhaps matched only by Durga Puja. Ajay Bose was a class by himself. At times, he would start describing a flotilla of clouds sailing across the azure winter sky, and so enchanted would he become with his own eloquence that he would forget all about the match for a few overs.

The first of January in 1967 was also the second day of a five-day test match between India and the famed West Indies led by Garfield Sobers, (I haven't added *Sir* before his name because it was long before he was knighted.) My dad and me got into the stadium after standing in a queue for hours. As we were excitedly waiting for the game to begin, we noticed some minor fracas happening between some spectators and policemen present in the stadium.

Soon, some policemen started beating spectators with lathis and the situation quickly went completely out of hand as people retaliated with whatever they could find, including bamboo poles taken from the fences. In an act of utter panic and maybe, stupidity, policemen burst tear gas shells in that enclosed space. Some enterprising men picked up the tear gas cans and threw them back at the cops. Tears rolled down my burning eyes as Father took me out before most people realised what was happening. We walked briskly and then took a taxi back home. Outside, there was little sign of what was happening within the stadium.

We got the full picture only from the papers next morning. There had been large-scale rioting; some spectators even pulled down tarpaulin covers over galleries and set them on fire. Some of the West-Indies players, who were running in terror along the Red Road, were rescued by policemen. They had good reasons to run. Mobs pelted stones randomly and several buses had been burned in Calcutta that day. But possibly, a much greater tragedy had been averted: as more than 50,000 people tried to exit through narrow gates, thousands could have died in stampede.

* * *

Besides sports, there wasn't much entertainment for children. Movies were rare gusts of happiness limited to *Ten Commandments*, *Ben Hur*, or *Do Aankhe Baara Haath*. Yes. I saw just three films until I began watching Hindi films on the sly when I was in high school. In the process, I fell in love with multiple female actors and became an irrevocable fan of Dev Anand,

Theatres, always freshly painted, had comfortable seats. Just being in an upmarket cinema like Lighthouse or Metro was a treat. The first time I was in Metro, it felt strange because my feet sank in an ankle-deep cushioned carpet. The city outside too had many elements that would impress a child.

The Calcutta I grew up in had cleaner roads and smaller crowds. Roads were manually swept and washed with water jets every morning. Hardly any structure was taller than three storeys, so the sky looked bigger. Footpaths were paved with rough stones. There were hawkers, but they were yet to take over the pavements. In the evening, gas lights would be lit in lovely little parks that were seen perhaps only in a dream. It was a joy to walk on the streets of the city.

Children were not the centre of the family. Grown-ups listened to the radio and wrote letters. A man would be measured by what he had in his head rather than how much he had in the bank. It took longer to travel across the city, but people lived closer to each other. Even the rich went to government hospitals where treatment was free. Some of the best schools too were government-run. Usha Uthup sang at the Trincas. The city known as Calcutta was still one of the finest in the world. Most importantly, people believed things would get better.

Plastic was yet to become omnipresent. Milk, medicines, and shampoos were sold in glass bottles. Bread and biscuits were wrapped in moisture-proof paper. Most products, from soaps to electric bulbs came in just a few brands. Newspapers had fewer adverts. It was unimaginable that the entire first page or the first few pages of a daily would carry adverts. Most importantly, there was no TV or mobile phone.

Almost nothing was thrown away when they became unusable: from shoes to thermos flasks. A whole lot of tradesmen earned their living by extending lifespans of everyday commodities.

In the last 70 years, more gadgets have become part of our lives than what had in the previous 70,000 years, during the period when homo Sapiens are believed to have spread from Africa to the entire world and brought themselves close to destruction. Cars, fridges, and air-conditioners existed in India then, but were unavailable to most people. Ceramic cookers, microwave ovens, pressure cookers, washing machines, dishwashers, mobile phones, computers/laptops, the internet and so on, which are taken for granted now were in an unimaginable future then.

Technology has irrevocably changed the way we think. For example, in the present time, no one will ever write like the Bengali poet Naresh Guha:

> If upon return to Kolkata
> As I whispered her name,
> The evening mail brought in her letter –
> If she herself came?

Part II
The University of Life

38 | How Green Was My Campus!

I was around 13 then. One evening, my father called me to his office to meet a visitor, something he rarely did. The visitor was an artist.

The gentleman, who was my father's age, saw my drawing book and a few watercolours on handmade paper. He also asked me a few questions about how I painted. Then he went on to discuss painting, landscapes, and the beauty of rural Bengal. He was talking with just a kid who dabbled in painting, but it was no baby talk. Looking back, I think it was unusual for a grown-up to treat a child as someone worthy of a serious discussion on fine arts.

Something he said that evening got etched in my head forever: 'If you wish to paint landscapes, see the countryside. And do visit Birbhum. Unless you've seen the Birbhum district, you won't have known the beauty of rural Bengal.'

Another artist, Subhash Kar (*A Face in the Crowd*), connected with children as equals. Long ago when I was very small, Subhas Kaku had accompanied our family on a trip to Santiniketan, where his estranged family possibly lived. When the artist in my dad's study insisted that I see Birbhum, I had faded memories of a quiet, enchanting place that was neither rural nor urban. Hidden in greenery, the homes there were unadorned yet beautiful in a quiet understated way. However, as a thirteen-year-old, I didn't know that Rabindranath Tagore's ashram school Visva-Bharati in Santiniketan was in the district of Birbhum. Neither did I know that after independence, Visva-Bharati had been turned into a Central University by the Nehru government in 1951. And naturally, I had no inkling that I would spend some of the happiest years of my life in the midst of the enchanting greenery there. In a sultry rainless July afternoon, I got off a train with a suitcase and a bedroll at Bolpur station to join an undergrad course at Visva-Bharati. A cycle rickshaw took me to a boys' hostel five kilometres away.

In 1968, Santiniketan hadn't changed much from the memory of the shaded countryside that had been engraved in my mind. The campus was green and indeed looked like an ashram. The architecture of the mostly one-storey buildings there bore the mark of an artist. I didn't know then, many of the iconic structures in the campus had been designed by Surendranath Kar, who had begun his career as a fine arts teacher in Tagore's school and became an architect later. Surendranath often accompanied Tagore on his tours abroad and on his return, applied what he had learned in different parts of the world. In the process, he created a new, distinctly Indian style of architecture that incorporated elements of style from different countries. You cannot miss the fact if you look at the old buildings of Santiniketan carefully.

The brick-and-mortar structures blended with the flora beautifully; countless trees almost concealed many of the buildings. The boys' hostel in front of the university canteen (somewhat pompously called the International Students' Canteen) too merged with the backdrop. The hostel had 11 small one-storey structures in a large compound with lots of tall leafy trees. Ten of them housed boy students, and the eleventh was a common room with a table tennis board, a few carrom boards, and a radio. My friend Gautam would be in the common room every Wednesday at 8 PM to listen to Radio Ceylon where Ameen Sayani had become a legend in his lifetime by presenting Hindi film songs in Binaca Geetmala. He would go on to host the programme for 40 years, possibly a world record for an individual radio presenter. (The incongruous phrase *radio jockey* hadn't been invented.)

Suitcase in hand, as I climbed the three steps leading to our hostel block, I was on a wide veranda with a low parapet that was broad enough to sit on. In front of me was the door to a room with four rudimentary wooden cots with stands for mosquito nets and four desks with armless chairs. Two uncovered yellow filament bulbs hung from the ceiling; there was no fan. Two smaller rooms that housed three boys each flanked the room in the centre.

A year of reckless ecstasy began.

39| An Undercover Hero

When I moved into the large room at the centre of the three-room hostel block, Gautam, Najful, and Swapan had already been there. Najful Haque, a quiet fellow, possibly found his roommates too boisterous for his taste. He shifted to another room. Sudip replaced him.

Swapan, who had graduated from school with distinction three years before, hadn't enrolled in college because his family couldn't afford it. He was a natural leader and a captivating speaker whose deep voice was incongruous with his wiry little figure. (Later, the voice would be put to good use for leading slogans during students' agitations.) If anything special was needed to be done, like cutting a green coconut, repairing a table clock, or breaking open a lock, Swapan would do it with ease. We soon became his followers.

The freedom offered by the unwalled campus and the relative lack of restraints meant we would spend a year of uninterrupted fun and frolic interspersed by exams. (Then, Gautam and I would shift to another hostel.) Once, around ten of us got into playing cards in groups of three or four. What began as a few games before studies in the evening expanded to fill the evening until supper. Then we decided we could play just a game or two before going to bed. The session soon stretched to midnight. A few days later, we got up in the morning and by an unspoken agreement, played a few games before class. Gradually, a time came when, we didn't attend classes at all and played cards round the clock with just the unavoidable breaks. After a brief period of collective insanity, one morning, we burned all the cards and never touched another for as long as we were on campus. The epidemic of playing cards ended as abruptly as it had begun, just as an epidemic ended in José Saramago's *Blindness.*

A few months after we moved into the hostel, there was an urgent summon for Swapan from the Principal's office. When Swapan didn't return for hours we felt something was amiss. When he did come back, he told us an untold story.

He had actually enrolled in Presidency College in Calcutta three years ago and would have graduated by then if …

* * *

The Presidency College, set up as Hindu College 151 years before, had been a seat of learning that attracted the best talents from Bengal and beyond. Their list of alumni was (and still is) virtually a who's who in Bengal: from the doyen of Indian science Sir Prafulla Chandra Ray to the physicists Satyendra Nath Bose and Meghnad Saha (who were classmates) to poet Jibanananda Dash to statistician Prashanta Chandra Mahalanobis to filmmaker Satyajit Ray. Subhash Chandra Bose, who cut his political teeth there, was expelled from the college in 1916 for manhandling a British prof scornful of Indians. The first President of independent India, Babu Rajendra Prasad too came to study F.A. (First Arts) at the college from Patna. Impressed by his intellect, an examiner once commented on his answer sheet: The "*examinee is better than examiner*"[xxvii]. A.K. Fazlul Haque, a "prime minister" of undivided Bengal in British India and arguably one of the greatest Bengali politicians, too had been an alumnus of Presidency. It was perhaps the only college in the subcontinent that had nurtured a future president of India and a future prime minister of Pakistan, Hussain Saheed Suhrawardy.

Therefore, besides being a centre of academic excellence, Presidency College (a university since 2010) had been a fertile nursery of politicians. The latest in the long list was the charismatic Ashim Chatterjee, who joined the college in 1960 to study physics but graduated in economics in 1965, and then continued there as a student leader. It was perhaps not surprising that his much younger classmates and juniors called him Kaka (Uncle)! Kaka, along with Santosh Rana, another Presidency alumnus who discontinued his

PhD studies at Rajabazar Science College of Calcutta University, led a large number of students into the Naxalbari (or Naxalite) movement that began in 1967 under the leadership of Jangal Santhal, Kanu Sanyal, and Charu Majumdar, about which I have mentioned in passing.

Their political allegiance was to communism in general and to the Chinese model of peasant revolution in particular. Their aim was to organise the poor, primarily the peasantry, for an armed revolution that would abolish the Indian state and create an egalitarian order. Liberal democracy, they reckoned, was a sham, and the parliament, as Lenin had famously said, was a pigsty. The Naxalites were also tired of the traditional Left leadership who, they felt, had become a part of the establishment and offered no solution to the stupendous problems of poverty or inequity.

Soon, one of the theoreticians of the original agitation, Charu Majumdar established himself as the supreme leader of the Naxalites. His words became unchallenged policy. Under his confounding leadership, the undertaking to create a new world would soon deviate from organising peasant struggles and degenerate into a mindless bloodbath. Majumdar figured that the easiest way to involve the poor in the agitation would be to kill rich people and policemen one by one. Unfortunately, his followers couldn't reach the big fish, so their default targets were minor moneylenders and landowners who treated the poor shabbily. Amongst policemen, their most common, no-sweat victim was the traffic constable. The police began paying back in kind and killed what seems to me the cream of our generation in Bengal. With hindsight, I am inclined to believe Charu Majumdar was insane. (I am not a psychiatrist; I'm using the word consciously in the sense it's commonly understood.)

Moving back to Swapan's story, the idea of an egalitarian India was hardly considered insane then. There was hope in the air and dream in the eyes of the young. Swapan too had got into the mix and left studies, along with many of his classmates, to work as a full-time activist in a remote village in Midnapur.

In 1968, when he wished to restart his academic career, Swapan didn't disclose his background to the university. When his past surfaced, courtesy the proactive police network, our Vice-Chancellor was Professor Kalidas Bhattacharya, a renowned scholar of philosophy. By and large, our teachers were liberal souls who had high tolerance for extreme political views, but there were a few who were after Swapan's blood. Who doesn't know that after matricide and incest, the greatest crime is suppressing information from authorities?

In the normal course of business, Swapan would have been expelled. But Professor Bhattacharya thought differently. He told Swapan to get a certificate from the Presidency College that there had been no complaint of misconduct against him. The Vice-Chancellor even said he would telephone the Principal of Presidency College and brief him on the matter.

Even after such an unexpected and incredibly generous offer, Swapan sat motionless, head bowed. Professor Bhattacharya looked at him for a long moment and asked, 'You don't have any cash, do you?'

He actually gave Swapan ₹20, a princely sum that would cover his trip to a city a hundred miles away.

40| A Legend's Home

Those days, there were only three modes of transport at our campus, Santiniketan: cycles, cycle rickshaws, and walking. (The second one has been replaced now by its new avatar, a battery-powered vehicle called "toto".) Even elderly professors used bicycles; in summer, they would wear a wide-brimmed hat made of palm leaves for protection against the scorching sun at latitude 23.68° N. Nobody owned a car. Besides a few Ambassadors for official use by the university, there was only one car on the campus. A 1933 Humber sedan—the number plate read WBA 8689—kept in a glass enclosure at what used to be the residence of Visva-Bharati's founder once. It's a museum now.

Three years before he passed away, Rabindranath Tagore bought the Humber for £400 (approximately ₹5,300). A journalist and automobile enthusiast, Joydip Sur has written on his blog that in the last years of his life, "Tagore just loved the car and would take a spin several times a day." Also,

> The 1933 Humber was perhaps the only car that Nobel Laureate Rabindranath Tagore ever called his own. He loved the car and used it till his last days. Beside the bard (sic), this historic car has had illustrious passengers like Netaji Subhas Chandra Bose, Mahatma Gandhi, Acharya Jagadish Chandra Bose and Jawaharlal Nehru.[xxviii]

Regarding a more recent Santiniketan, I have written: "Hidden in greenery, the homes there were unadorned yet beautiful in a quiet, understated way." Subtle taste, whether in architecture, artefacts, or about quotidian objects, is not acquired from books or in classrooms; it has to be gained through experience. The converse too is true. If a guy who loves fiery hooch is offered fine wine, he might feel cheated. (I may sound snooty, but once I received such a guest, regrettably.)

Soon after joining Visva-Bharati, we had a little experiential learning on how the ordinary could be turned elegant.

The distance between our department and hostel was two kilometres, which we would cover on foot until a few of us acquired bicycles that would soon become common property. One afternoon while we were returning to our hostel, it started pouring; we got into the nearest compound to stand in the covered veranda in front of the house. Houses in Santiniketan didn't have porticos (as nobody had a car). However, almost every house had a covered veranda outside with a low and wide parapet wall that would also serve as seats, like in our hostel. Residents often received visitors in that area, and it was commonly used in lieu of a drawing room for adda.

A little later, a lady in her forties opened the door and asked us to sit inside. Although there were a few settees and some wicker stools in the room, we couldn't sit down. The cushions on them had such delicate tapestry that by an unspoken agreement, we decided not to sully the fine works of art by placing our nether ends on them. We just admired them. And also, the paintings on the walls.

We didn't know that the house belonged to Nandalal Bose (1882-1966), who had been a leading light of modern Indian painting.

Nandalal had developed the fine arts school in Santiniketan—Kala Bhaban into a premier institution. Some of the paintings in that room were possibly the master's original masterpieces! The lady who offered us the wicker stools was one of his daughters, Gouridi or Yamunadi.

Having come this far, you would know that in Bangla, we use the suffix -di for an older sister, and -da, for an older brother. You would also have noticed that the usage is not limited to siblings or cousins. We often use it to address an older friend, colleague, or neighbour. Santiniketan stretched the idea a little far. There, everyone was a -da or a -di to anyone who was younger. It was normal for a seventeen-year-old freshman to address a doyen in her sixties by adding -di to her first name.

So, it is normal for me to refer to Nandalal Bose's daughters using the fraternal suffix although I met them only once, that too for moments. Nandalal had passed two years before we joined Visva-Bharati in Santiniketan, but there were several living legends at the campus. One evening, we saw Rabindranath Tagore's daughter-in-law, Pratima Devi sitting at an outer veranda of their residence Konark in the Uttarayan complex (not far from where the Humber sat). She was looking into the distance. Exceedingly fair and beautiful, she seemed to be from another world.

41| A Door Unopened

The celebrities who lived in Santiniketan when we were studying there included the gifted classical musician Dhrubatara Joshi, painter extraordinaire Binode Behari Mukherjee, a sculptor of rare brilliance, Ramkinkar Baij, and the fabled singer of Tagore songs, Kanika Bandyopadhyay. Each one of them was special, let me write a little about two of them.

Born in a modest family in the arid district of Bankura in West Bengal, Ramkinkar (1906-1980) had been an accomplished self-taught artist when destiny brought him to Santiniketan. His genius was recognized by both his teacher Nandalal and Tagore himself. Although he came to Santiniketan for a few years to hone his skills, Ramkinkar ended up spending his life there.

Traditionally, sculptures in India depicted gods and kings and were either carved in stone or cast in bronze. Going off the beaten track, Ramkinkar sculpted concrete statues of peasant families with strong Santhal features, some of which have become milestones in the history of modern Indian sculpture. The Yaksha and Yakshini in front of the Reserve Bank of India in New Delhi are examples of his virtuosity. (He also sculpted many images of Hindu gods, particularly Saraswati, the goddess of learning.) Ramkinkar, who was called Kinkarda by one and all following the local custom, lived with his Santhal partner, Radha Rani. Their relationship was reluctantly tolerated by the conservative and somewhat reactionary social milieu of Santiniketan, but never accepted.

Although he was a faculty member of the university and had been a guru to many a leading sculptor of our time, Ramkinkar lived in a crumbling mud cottage—perhaps the only house in Santiniketan that didn't have a fence. Ramkinkar, didn't fit into the mould of an average person; he lived in his very personal world of creativity. In 1970, he was awarded the Padma Bhushan, a civilian honour in India. In the function held to felicitate him, Ramkinkar—a little tipsy as usual—kept smiling sweetly throughout. He also sang a romantic song when the audience demanded it, but had to be reminded the lines. The real artist in him came out when he was asked to say something about his latest honour. His speech went like this.

'There was a telegram from Delhi, "Padma Shri awarded, accepted or not?"'

Padma Shri too is a civilian honour, but at a lower order in the hierarchy of national awards. The audience spoke out in unison, 'No Kinkarda, you've been awarded Padma Bhushan, not Padma Shri.'

Ramkinkar Baij, unfazed: 'Oh yes, Padma Bhushan. Does it matter? They wrote, "Padma Bhushan awarded, accepted or not?" I wrote back, "Why not?" and they gave it!'

A memoir written by Somendranath Bandyopadhyay, a former professor of Visva-Bharati and a Tagore scholar, who I was fortunate to know personally, mentions an anecdote in his book *Artist Ramkinkar, in Conversation.* One day, Ramkinkar went to the only commercial bank on the campus to cash a fixed deposit. Somendranath writes[xxix]:

> The young bank clerk tries to explain, 'Kinkarda, you opened the fixed deposit account just the other day. It will mature after six years. How can you get the money now?' Kinkarda nods gloomily, 'Yes, I know, I know. It matures after six years.' 'Then why did you take the trouble to come in today?' the clerk asked with a smile. In all seriousness, Kinkarda said, 'True. But I just wondered, what if it had matured suddenly? Thought I'd check.'

Unlike Ramkinkar Baij, Kanika Bandyopadhyay (1924-2000), known as "Mohordi" to everyone on the campus, lived an ordinary middle-class life. Long after I graduated, once I accompanied a friend to her simple, unadorned Santiniketan home, the official residence of a professor of music. I was amazed to meet a person who was a household name for millions of Bengalis the world over to be so unassuming. Wearing a simple blue cotton sari, she talked to us as if she were any other homemaker receiving guests. An ex-student of Visva-Bharati from Bangladesh was with her then, as a stay-in student in the guru-shishya tradition of ancient India. The shishya is a leading Bengali singer today, Rezwana Choudhury Bannya.

As we are talking about famous people, let me add another name, although he never lived in Santiniketan, Abdul Ghaffar Khan, the founder of Khudai Khidmatgar, the peaceful Pashtun struggle against British colonialists. One of the tallest leaders of our freedom struggle and a personal friend of Gandhi, Ghaffar Khan visited India in 1969 for Gandhiji's birth centenary celebrations. The trip was a sad reality check for him; he saw first-hand how independent India had tossed his friend away. He didn't hesitate to express his anguish in public meetings.

After reaching Bolpur station late on 13 December 1969 by train, Ghaffar Khan spent a cold night on a coach shunted to the siding. Next morning, the Chief Minister of West Bengal, Ajay Mukherjee accompanied him to Santiniketan. He was taken to the room where he had spent a day with Tagore 35 years before. Visva-Bharati felicitated him.

I was not there at the function at the mango orchard in

Santiniketan. Neither did I meet Ramkinkar Baij ever. But I saw him from a distance often; big-built and absentminded, he was always in a shabby shirt and a lungi. Some of the frescos of Binode Behari, which are acknowledged to be masterpieces in modern Indian art, were in Cheena Bhavan and Hindi Bhavan right across our hostel. I saw them, but didn't realise what treasure they were. And I didn't have any idea that Dhrubatara Joshi, who had been a rising sitarist along with Ravi Shankar and Vilayet Khan, had had his promising career cut short by a cerebral infraction. Otherwise, the revered music teacher could have been a famous performing artist.

Founded by one of the tallest Indian thinkers, Santiniketan nurtured some exceptional minds, from Syed Mujtaba Ali, Satyajit Ray and Balraj Sahni to Mahasweta Devi, KG Subramanian and Amartya Sen, besides the names I have already mentioned. When I went there in the late 1960s, academically, Visva-Bharati was an unexceptional university that no longer lived up to her motto to "bring the world together in a single nest," but Santiniketan was a special part of our cultural heritage all the same.

There was an invisible door between the two realities that anyone could open with a little effort. Sadly, I never tried to open it.

42| Dissimilar Revolutionaries

Despite studying at Visva-Bharati, I didn't really acquaint myself with the facets of Santiniketan that made it a unique centre of cultural heritage. The reason was partly my naivety and partly, the political atmosphere of the time. Communism, like every other religion, demands absolute, undivided allegiance from its followers. The idea got into our head that much of Santiniketan deserved to be shunned. We "othered" a lot of people.

Under the charismatic leadership of the undercover hero Swapan, some of us got sucked into a political movement that attracted eighteen-year-olds but was destined to fail. In the process, we drifted away from a rich cultural ambience that was right on the other side of an invisible door which I have just described.

However, with the benefit of hindsight stretching over five decades, I can say that being an insignificant part of a failed rebellion wasn't really a bad idea. The experience opened to us the doors to homes of poor peasants, which wouldn't have happened otherwise. The experience also taught me to respect every human being irrespective to their station in life, which is not minor education in a country dominated by a diabolical caste system for two millennia.

I was exceedingly fond of Kalida, the head cook at our hostel kitchen, who was tall, dark, and big. He also sported a paunch under his white singlet. By some magic, the ever-smiling Kalida always had a seven-day-old stubble. Another kitchen employee I was fond of was Dwijada, a diminutive man who always looked worried. Kalida lived in a storeroom behind the kitchen smelling of onion and garlic. Dwijada cycled from his home in a nearby village every morning and went back after a fourteen-hour workday. Despite their differences in sizes, looks, and lodgings, they both earned ₹45 a month besides free meals. You can appreciate how paltry the sum was when you compare the amount with the ₹65 that every boarder paid for two meals for a month at the same kitchen.

If you wish to understand the grotesque inequalities of India, you just have to look around. Twenty years after Visva-Bharati became a central government university, which conferred benefits like structured pay-scales, pension, free healthcare, etc., to its teachers and all other employees, around 40 workers in the kitchens for students at different colleges earned a pittance with nothing to fall back upon in the autumn of their life. Their working conditions used to be what it was for workers before they earned eight-hour workdays after persistent struggles in Europe and America through the 19th century.

Our kitchen workers were marked as "casual workers" in the records of the university, although their work was anything but casual! They had been petitioning the university for regular pay, working hours, and working clothes for many years without success. After enrolling in Visva-Bharati, Swapan took over the job of writing their petitions with the help of a local lawyer and a trade union leader. As petitioning didn't work, the kitchen employees decided to go on a flash strike two days before an annual winter festival when lots of parents and other visitors were expected to have meals at our kitchens. A little arm-twisting helps when you are cornered. The kitchen staff got two sets of uniform within two days. They were absorbed as regular employees within months.

With a little help from Swapan, the process was repeated for all the 320 "casual" labourers like gardeners and cleaning staff at the university. However, like my schoolmate Samir who didn't realise his potential to become a footballer, Swapan didn't fulfil his promise of becoming a political leader either. He has lived a quiet life of a school teacher, but with a major difference. Not many teachers could write on their CV—if they wished to—that they made a major difference to the lives of 360-odd families.

Here, I must add that the Vice-Chancellor and the Registrar (the administrative head of the university), were not unsympathetic to the employees; they had suffered not because of a lack of compassion in the hearts of powerful men, but because of oversight.

* * *

Getting involved in student politics also gave me the opportunity to become an admirer and friend of Tarapada Guha, which was not his real name. Despite the fact that I knew him by a fake name for many years of our friendship, he was one of the most genuine humans I have come across in life. He remained a close friend until he died a few years ago because of colon cancer and malnourishment.

Tarapada, a few years older than me, was a political activist who worked on the other side of the law. He too was a Naxalite, but belonged to a group that didn't believe killing individuals could lead to revolution. His political group, too tiny to be called a party, aspired to bring in a revolution by organising peasants patiently. Tarapada had left a relaxed job in Calcutta to become a full-time political worker in Birbhum, where he didn't have an address. He moved around in an area of maybe 500 square kilometres with all his earthly possessions in a jhola slung on shoulder and a country-made pistol strapped to his waist. He slept in homes of peasants.

Tarapada, a cheerful person, packed tremendous stamina in his slender body. I accompanied him a couple of times as I enjoyed the company of this unusual man in an even more unusual career. Once, after spending a night under a tree at a peasant household in the company of countless stars and mosquitoes, Tarapada and I began walking towards his next destination at dawn. It was about three in the afternoon when we reached a place where my host was able to cook some rice and a few bland potatoes. It was one of the most satisfying meals of my life.

Although Tarapada carried a pistol, he was one of the gentlest souls I knew. Never a leader, he was a comrade always; and he worked under the leadership of hollow men. That he was under the constant threat of being killed by policemen or their hired goons in the killing fields of Bengal in the early 1970s didn't make him surly.

On the contrary, he attracted one and all with his charming personality.

When the revolution failed, Tarapada Guha vanished and Pradeep Chatterjee of Sahitya Parishad Street of North Calcutta resurfaced as a meter inspector in Calcutta Electric Supply Corporation, thanks to the trade union he had once discarded. But on that day, Fate smiled one of her oft-mentioned nasty smiles. A clerical error made him 10 years older in the company records. Consequently, he had to retire at the age of 50. By then, he had married and got a daughter.

The following 14 years of his life would be another uninterrupted struggle, but this time, for a simpler cause, to keep the fire going in his kitchen. Incidentally, he would also be cheated of his life's savings by a close relative. But that is another story.

43| Lambu: A Blast from the Past

After many decades, I saw packets of lambus in Pintu's street-corner grocery near our Kolkata home. It took me on a rather long journey down memory lane.

Having been an average student, I don't expect my teachers to remember me. Recently at a party, I met one of our several wonderful professors. This gentleman had been an exceedingly handsome young man, and not much older than us. He was a minor hero for us boys, and a major heartthrob for the girls, much to our irritation. (Why are contests in life so bloody unequal?) Anyway, to cut a long story short, when I introduced myself in the gathering, my former teacher looked at me so helplessly that I felt sorry for him. I ought not to have revealed my identity and challenged his memory so bluntly.

My years at our university campus was by far the most gorgeous period of my life, although it was not devoid of minor deprivations. Although our hostel kitchen provided two large meals for an entire month in exchange for 65 to 75 paper-gold rupees, we had to fend for the breakfast and afternoon snacks ourselves. We managed the breakfast somehow and stuffed ourselves during lunch, but we would be famished by five in the afternoon.

If I may share with you a bit about our financial situation, we used to invest a sizable chunk of our meagre monthly allowance on the two local cinemas, cups of tea, and packets of Charminar. Charminar was possibly the strongest cigarette in the world without the embellishment of a filter. Not even Marlboro (supposedly the cowboy's favourite), was nearly as robust. Consequently, we often found our rather healthy afternoon appetite an insurmountable budget deficit.

On days we were lucky, we would find one of our distant girlfriends in the university cafeteria. For our generation of boys, it was an immense good fortune that girls didn't smoke then. So, they always had a little cash to spare, and would often volunteer to keep us alive by offering a samosa or two.

But on days we were not lucky, we had to eat something. After serious research, we found the most cost-effective snack, which would have been cheaper than twenty-five paise then.

It was the LAMBU!

If you have a nodding acquaintance with Hindi or Bangla, you would be aware that a tall lad is often called a Lambu in these languages. Amitabh Bachchan has been the reigning Lambu in his spectacular film career. Therefore, I will die without solving the mystery how the rotund stuff came to be known as "lambu".

Lambu is neither biscuit nor cake. Genetically, I believe, it is closer to the popular Bihari/Jharkhandi snack litthi, which has a hard central core and an even harder shell. Woe betide a person with less than healthy teeth trying to bite a lambu! But that was only a minor problem for the indigent lambu eaters. More problematically, the lambu would be baked with the cheapest fat available in the market, possibly animal fat discarded by butchers. Therefore, as you ate it, a fatty layer got smudged to the inside of your mouth. But we took that too in our stride. Munch a lambu and wash it down with a glass of water, and you won't have to eat anything in the next four hours. Trust me!

The packets of lambus in Pintu's grocery brought back all these memories in a flash. I couldn't but buy one and taste it. It was yesterday once more. Here's my report.

The lambu hasn't changed one jot. The same hardness, same lingering fatty taste, the same earthy granules which wouldn't be mentioned in the recipe. … It was perfect.

I can safely skip lunch today!

44| Just One Circle

In Bangla, dash (it rhymes with cosh) stands for ten and chakra, for wheel or circle. (Remember the Sudarshan Chakra, the spinning-disc missile in the hand of the Hindu god Krishna? Or its modern version which Vijay Amritraj used in the James Bond film *Octopussy*?) Chakra also means conspiracy. Together, *dashachakra* means a conspiracy hatched by many, that is, an intrigue or machination. However, the Dashachakra Hostel, where I moved into in my second year of stay in Santiniketan had nothing to do with intrigues, neither did it have 10 circles.

It had just one circular courtyard at the centre shaded by two ancient mango trees, around which were 10 two-bed rooms and a bathroom block. The rooms opened into the circular courtyard. The rectangular rooms had two beds on the two longer sides and three windows each. One of the windows was in the far wall, directly opposite the door; the other two were on either side.

The architecturally beautiful wheel-shaped edifice stood about 50 feet off a straight road on which only cycles and cycle-rickshaws plied. The foreground was barren. A slightly raised straight path of red gravel connected Dashachakra to the road.

On the other side of the road was the main playground of the campus. So, from the entrance of the hostel, we would see an enormous open space which merged into the greenery on the far side.

Behind Dashachakra, there was another small boys' hostel called the Punjabi House—a reminder of a time when Santiniketan was a more cosmopolitan place—and a few staff quarters, where teachers lived with families. Behind them were paddy fields. The proximate presence of professors was a nuisance, needless to say.

With three large windows in every room, our hostel was airy and light. In fact, wind swept through it all the time. Thanks to the superb air circulation, the summer afternoons were quite bearable in Dashachakra, but the winter nights were really cold, when the temperature dipped below 10° Centigrade (plus the windchill factor!).

I was in a different hostel when I first went to Dashachakra in a frigid night. Shivering in cold despite two layers of woollens, as I walked towards the hostel, I saw a hairy man standing outside, looking into the distance, with nothing on his upper torso, and a printed red lungi below. I thought he was a madman. But he wasn't. He was Dilip Paul from Dhaka, East Pakistan, a few years my senior.

Dilip's roommate was Anuttam, who was a normal person, meaning he could feel cold. But Dilip would allow him to close only one and a half windows on his side of the room whatever might the temperature be and however piercing the wind. I do not know why Anuttam accepted the deal. Maybe, it was his Buddha-like tolerance or maybe, Dilip Paul had some special charm? The answer would be bits of both, I guess.

I was in that hostel for two years. The circular design of the building meant we would interact with each other closely. Did it contribute to making the place a more friendly one? I think yes.

The hostel had such a motley crowd! Let me begin with my roommate, Gautam. The badminton champion of the university, he also played football well despite smoking like a chimney and doing no physical training at all. Generous to a fault, Gautam would shower gifts on friends whenever he could afford it and at times, when he couldn't. If he was sharing food say a cutlet with a friend, he would surely part with the bigger "half" going against the trend. On the other hand, if a girl was paying for our tea and snacks at our self-service canteen—which wasn't rare—Gautam would volunteer to get the food, and afterwards, he would tell the girl in a serious voice, 'I'm keeping the change.'

Turning back to the hostel with 20 boys, two most disciplined and likable guys were the roommates Shil Chand and Nikhil. Besides participating in the National Cadet Corps drills diligently, they studied. They would study till late into the night when everyone else had gone to bed; the next morning, anyone who got up early would see them at their desks. I suspect Shil and Nikhil considered it a moral obligation to make up for the lack of efforts by some of their friends. Soumitra and Tapan were two of the gentlest souls I have met. Soumitra's handwriting was printed cursive writing and Tapan was the default tabla player for musical functions. Both were great fun to be with.

Our kitchen-cum-dining-hall was five minutes' walk from Dashachakra. One evening, as four or five of us were returning after supper, Tapan spotted a girl who he had never talked to, but had a serious crush on. He said, 'Give me a minute. I've been thinking of proposing to her for some time. Let me be done with it. কাজটা সেরে নিই।'

He walked briskly, accosted the girl, exchanged a few words with her and came back equally briskly, as if nothing had happened. That evening, we were witness to the briefest courtship in human history.

Dilip Paul, who studied chemistry, was a reader of impenetrable books. He was much older than his age and we would refer to him as Sri Paul, which would have been quite a weighty name for a twenty-something. Koushik and Siddhartha were two adorable younger students. Koushik, besides being a gifted student, had a whacky sense of humour; Siddhartha, who studied English, was an excellent tenor. Both of them would migrate to the US. From there, Siddhartha has left for a place much farther away. Above all, there was Anuttam, an unusual person and a brilliant singer and poet, who I will come back to. Finally, Badruddoza didn't have to live with the mystery that the rest of us were condemned to suffer from. He had been married.

Gopalda, an elderly man, cleaned our hostel. He was one of the 360-odd casual labourers who had had been absorbed as regular employees by the university, partly because of our friend Swapan's efforts. Gopalda looked very ancient and seemed way beyond the age of superannuation. When we quizzed him about his age, he would turn serious, 'My dad wrote down my date of birth on a chit of paper, but I've lost it.' When he developed some problem with his vision, one day he told me, "Will you give me one of your old specs?'

Anuttam's younger brother, Gautam, aka Bulti, moved into the hostel a year later. He immediately initiated a process to beautify the barren patch in front of our hostel. He didn't actually plant any trees; instead, he wrote long missives in convoluted officialese to the university gardening department, containing his wish list. To add more weight, Bulti got a peon book, numbered the letters, and sent them through Gopalda. Bulti insisted on stamped acknowledgements for all his letters.

The gardening department didn't bother initially, but Bulti would keep sending reminders: "It has been noted with serious disfavour that your goodselves do not consider it obligatory to look into the pressing aesthetic necessity to beautify the disagreeable barren patch in front of Dashachakra Hostel, and thereby betraying a lackadaisical attitude about …" etc. etc.

After some time, either because of Bulti's nerve-racking English or because of the peon book, the gardening department sent a cartload of manured soil and maybe 20 saplings and got them planted on either side of the gravelled path in front of our hostel.

Mission accomplished, we soon forgot all about the plants. One day, I saw Biren holding an uprooted plant upside down and observing it with utmost seriousness. Alexander Flemming wouldn't have looked at the petri dish containing the contaminated bacteria more intently when he first saw it. When I asked him what he was doing, Biren said, 'Checking how well the roots are growing.'

* * *

The playground in front of our hostel would fall asleep after dusk. On certain nights, when it became a sea of moonlight, a girl would push a wheelchair with her boyfriend, a paraplegic singer and a senior student at the music school, Sangeet Bhavan, to the edge of the field. M, who is an eminent singer now, would sing khayals or thumris that would submerge the area around our hostel in soulful music. We would speak in whispers in those times.

When I visited Santiniketan after 50 years, there was no Dashachakra. The building had been allowed to go to seed. Peepuls grew from its unattended crevices as plaster fell off. Then the university demolished the structure.

Fortunately, no authorities can ever demolish memories.

45| Celebrating Seasons

The happiest moment after joining college arrived a few weeks after our academic term began. The sky was overcast that morning; a wet wind was blowing away leaves and twigs, announcing the onset of happy rains. As we were reluctantly preparing for college, the news came it would be a day off for the entire university. Moreover, it would be a day of *outing*, an English word I hadn't heard.

Soon, hundreds of boys and girls began walking away from the university campus, along gravelled roads, across barren undulating red laterite grounds called the khowai, many singing in groups. Our destination was the River Kopai. The horizon beckoned us as dark clouds above turned the ground below into a darker shade of red. An outing was a part of the campus life in Santinketan. An event to usher in a new season.

Whoever had thought of the event was a teenager at heart. Apart from being close to nature, it was the first time I was in proximity with so many young girls. After nine years in a boys' school that was as barren as the sands of a seashore, spending half a day with so many beautiful girls was a delight. Countless glances would have been stolen that morning, and I guess some hearts would have been exchanged, or just given!

* * *

Wednesday is the weekly day off. On a Wednesday morning when it's still dark, about 10 of us decide to go on an unofficial outing. We begin walking across the campus aiming to catch the sun rising from behind the railway track. On the eastern edge of Santiniketan, along which the main railway line from Kolkata to North Bengal runs, the there is a natural elevation. As rail lines avoid steep climbs, a gorge was cut through the highland to lay the track. Therefore, as you walk in that direction, you come across a sudden, unexpected chasm, at the bottom of which is a railway track. Trains moving below look like toy trains from there. There was a bridge across the railway line once. Now, its broken abutments hang out desolately on either side. As the paths leading to the once-upon-a-time overpass too have been swept away by decades of dust, storm, and unuse, the two ends of the bridge look surreal now. One wonders what purpose the bridge with no pathways on either side ever served.

As darkness fades and the sun rises in the shivering autumn sky, the red soil below catches fire. At different levels of the sloping ground on either side of the rail line, clusters of white kash flowers beam at the fluffy clouds above as a clanging Darjeeling Mail runs below. When the sound of the train dies away, serenity regains her lost ground. Even the bunch of noisy teenaged boys stop talking. A cold breeze blows, sending occasional shivers down my spine.

Someone puts an ear on a hollow steel telegraph post and calls others. We take turns to listen to the gorgeous oceanic sound that reverberates within the pole. The memory of that sound is etched in stone in my mind. Rabindranath Tagore would have written the following lines in a morning like this, I guess.

I've travelled widely, over much time
Spending amounts that were not a dime
I've seen mountains
Have been to oceans;
But I haven't taken a few steps
To see the dewdrop on paddy leaves.

The calming effect of the sublime autumn sunrise ended abruptly when, on our way back, we noticed a small guava tree laden with fruits in front of the main girls' hostel. For a change, we forgot everything about the girls within and allowed ourselves to be lost to the eternal charm of semi-ripe guavas. No one said anything, but instinctively, all of us got into the hostel compound and began pillaging guavas. We would have left in minutes, but couldn't because the warden of the hostel, a largish lady and reputed martinet, stomped out and confronted us: 'What are you doing? Don't you have any shame? Are you from decent families? What do you think your parents will say when they are informed? How can you create such a ruckus in front of a girls' hostel? …'

Facing a relentless barrage of angry rhetorical questions, we did the best thing that we could under the circumstances. We cringed, hung our heads in a collective display of shame, and waited for the storm to run its course. But there was no respite; the harangue went on and on.

Perhaps the lady had stopped for a moment to catch her breath when Gautam held up a small card wrapped in plastic and said politely, but loudly enough for everyone to hear, 'Madam, we have our ID cards.'

Our tormentor simply said, 'Goh!' and turned back. Never ever have I seen power and authority being confronted (and confused) with such complete nonsense.

46| Night Out: The Bridge on the River Kopai

Whoever thinks Hindi is the Indian language that has the most colourful profanities hasn't met my friend Subroto Hajra from a village near Sainthia in a western corner of West Bengal. Subroto—friends call him Bonu—could reel out an astonishing array of Bangla swearwords at a breakneck speed. But only if someone rubbed him on the wrong side; otherwise, he was a genial soul. Before moving on to the story of a foolish midnight adventure with Bonu, let me tell you how Subrata became Bonu.

Among the several beautiful girls in our class was Anusri. She was charming, slender, and reserved. As she talked very little, she also had an aura of mystery around her. A year after sharing the classroom with her, one day, Subroto referred to her as Bonosree instead of Anusri. It was just a slip, but Subroto would not be forgiven for not knowing the name of one of the most beautiful girls around. He was dragged through the mud for the sin and was called Bonosree thereafter. In due course, the moniker mutated into Bonu.

Beneath Bonu's apparently abrasive exterior lived a poet. He didn't usually smoke, but sometime during his stay in our hostel, he acquired a few packets of long Kent cigarettes that had even longer white filter tips. He hid this treasure securely from predators in a locked box in a locked steel trunk. But at times, when the night was particularly beautiful, he would ask me to accompany him on a walk. But the pretext would be different; he would always say, borrowing the manufacturer's advertising slogan: 'Let's have a Kent!'

Once, in a cloudless full-moon night, Bonu suddenly proposed we go for a long walk. The two of us set out with a flask containing black Nescafé and a pack of Kents. It was a foolish thing to do because the time was early 1970s when the Naxalite movement was at its peak in our district; young people were killed randomly with no questions asked. Armed policemen patrolled roads at night. Among them were specimens who would shoot a suspect before talking.

We walked across the old fairground and then towards the north as the world slept on either side of the eerily empty road. After crossing the irrigation canal near Shyambati, we turned right. The vast empty tract of undulating land before us was washed by a gossamer silvery light as water gurgled in the canal flowing alongside. We crossed the empty patch of barren land that served as an open-air crematorium for the villages around. Scattered remains of burnt wood and memories of the few men and women who we had accompanied in their last journey made our feet heavier.

We went past the tiny Prantik station, which was fast asleep, and continued along a walking trail that ran parallel to the railway track. The trail ended when we reached the Kopai. On the other side of the slender river before us, we could see the solitary light of the even tinier Kopai station far away. That station had hardly anyone even in daytime.

The almost dry, dark riverbed lay much below with a stream or two of gleaming molten silver shining in the moonlight. It was that time of the year when there was hardly any water in Kopai. The absolute silence wasn't broken by even an owl's hoot. It was pure bliss; we were not going anywhere; our aim was to cross the bridge and go as far as our legs would take us.

The narrow bridge across Kopai was just a single rail track on spans of girders resting on four or five piers. There was nothing above: no truss, not even railings. There was no pathway alongside. To cross the bridge, one had to walk on wooden sleepers, which have vanished like our childhood. As we were crossing the distance of about a hundred metres, gusts of wind swept our faces.

We were halfway down the bridge, walking leisurely, when a sudden, strong beam of light blinded us. A train was hurtling towards us from the opposite side, accompanied by a deafening noise. The dry riverbed lay 30 to 40 feet below. There was no way we could turn back and outrun the train. Should we jump off?

On bridges like these, railways construct small square platforms by the side of the line at fixed intervals. Later, a railway engineer friend of mine told me it is called a *trolley refuge*; it's used to keep push-trolleys when required. A little ahead of us on the left, there was a trolley refuge, which was the unlikely but only possible refuge for us, that is, if we were to see another sunrise.

As the bridge shook sadistically, we ran directly towards the rushing train as fast as we could, looking directly at its blazing Cyclops eye. We had to reach the platform before the train did, all the while hoping there would be no missteps. It was perhaps the longest 10 seconds of my life, but we managed to reach the platform, as you would have guessed.

But reaching the trolley refuge was not the end of our trouble. The platform shook more violently than the track, with an amplitude of maybe, a foot. We would have been thrown off if there hadn't been a steel parapet on three sides of the platform. We grabbed the railings and hung on for our dear life.

It was a goods train, which means it had at least 40 wagons. It took an eternity to cross the bridge as we danced on the platform, something like the present-day hip-hop. However, when the train finally crossed the bridge, before we could breathe out a sigh of relief, a new problem arose.

A strong beam of torchlight fell on us and we saw—to our horror—two armed policemen standing on the ledge behind the guard's coach, one holding the torch, and the other taking aim at us with a rifle. We jumped and lay down as fast as we could. Bonu, an avid NCC cadet, said under his breath, 'Three-naught-three.'

Whether he was correct or not in identifying the calibre of the gun, as we ducked, we would have been hidden from the policemen's view.

We were destined to see another sunrise.

47 | Moni

Soon after meeting Shubhendu Sekhar Mukhopadhyay, I became one of his numerous fans. When I was an undergraduate student, Shubhenduda was a research officer at Rabindra Bhaban, an institute in our university devoted to research into the life and works of Tagore. A bachelor, he lived on the campus in a sparsely furnished room in a one-storey university guesthouse. Even now, I can see it if I close my eyes. ... An approximately 16-feet by 12-feet room divided into two parts by a rudimentary cot in the middle, which had a stand for hanging a mosquito net. On one side was a desk and a bookshelf, and on the other, a kerosene stove on which he prepared his frugal meals, and often, tea for us. Shubhenduda had a mischievous sense of humour. Once he said, 'Despite 190 years of terrible colonial exploitation, I forgive the Brits for three reasons.'

This was not expected from a strongly left-leaning intellectual who wore khadi. Surprised, we asked, 'What are the reasons?'

'Cakes, chocolate, and ice creams.'

From the room, we could see an expanse of the sky and a red gravelled road lined by acacia and palash leading to the guesthouse. Through two large windows that were always open, light streamed in. The door too was usually open. Shubhenduda's dwelling was as open and inviting as his mind was.

* * *

Shubhendu Sekhar wrote brilliant Bangla, both prose and poetry. (He also wrote excellent English, but that I would learn much later.) It is unfortunate that he hasn't written much. His writings have recently been compiled in a slim volume. His short stories and poems are scintillating; his essays carry the stamp of an extremely erudite person.

Shubhenduda could speak with authority on lots of subjects. His knowledge, particularly of Rabindranath Tagore's life and works, was deep and wide. But if anyone seemed awestruck by his erudition, he would try to inverse the impression with a disarming smile and a caustic comment, 'I don't read books, I read only book covers and jackets. Only illiterates like you think I'm well-read.'

As I have written, we went through university during the turbulent time around 1970. The Naxalbari movement began, spread and died during the period, and along with it died thousands of young men, as the genteel Indian democracy bared its venomous fangs. It was a time when protests swept like bushfire through campuses from Berkeley to Sorbonne to Calcutta. Students' protests had led to the fall of the De Gaulle government in France in 1968. Shortly thereafter, Bangladesh achieved independence at a tremendous human cost. Through it all, the underdog Vietnam decisively won the most asymmetric war in human history. It was a time when hope was endemic. It was a time when younger people in India, except the jellyfish, believed in a cause. Mostly, a rebel cause.

Shubhenduda too was a rebel, in a very personal way. He lived like a hermit, was staunchly anti-establishment, but wasn't part of any organized political group (as far as I know). Maybe, he had foreseen the future of the Left movement in India. He was remarkably free from prejudices that many Indian leftists hold, as the anecdote about cakes and chocolate would have told you.

I lost touch with him as I took up a peripatetic job soon after graduation. Years later, after returning to Calcutta in 1983, I picked up the thread. By then, he had married Hena Deb, who is like an older sister to me, and they had a lovely daughter, Tinni.

Shubhenduda was the Head of the Sahitya Akademi for Eastern India and had an office at a quaint corner of the city, in the stadium complex beside the beautiful Dhakuria Lake, not far from my office. After office, I would often meet him and walk long distances with him, followed by coffee and upma at a South Indian eatery. He would never allow me to pay for the snacks. And on every single occasion, I came home with a feeling that he had thrown light on some dark corner of my mind.

Shubhenduda used to regale his audience with witty anecdotes. Besides a quirky sense of humour, he had a rare gift of repartee. Henadi is from the district of Sylhet, which is now in Bangladesh. The district was an early bird in spreading education, particularly women's education. People from the place were known for their intellectual snobbery and clannishness. Sylhet is also an area where the physiognomy of the people doesn't fit the conventional markers of beauty such as a sharp nose or large eyes. A country cousin of Henadi once said, 'Shubhendu babu, you must give it to us; no fool has ever been born in Sylhet.'

The reply was instantaneous: 'Nor a beauty!'

* * *

Shubhenduda was always in a sparkling white khadi dhoti and kurta. In their large sparsely furnished two-storey house in Park Circus, they ate sitting on floor and slept on hard beds. Shubhenduda had an impressive personal library, but had no fancy bookcases—only open unpainted wooden racks that went up to the ceiling. The walls were white and largely bare, save for a few paintings by Henadi, and a framed postcard written long back by his father's grandfather. Among other things, the postcard written in Bangla ordained, "Sell your land, sell your house if you have to, but study."

Their house was impeccably clean, always. Tinni doted on our two children, who were slightly younger, and together with her big black gentlemanly Labrador Prama, they were a happy foursome. Incidentally, in Bangla, the word prama means deep knowledge! For my wife and me, Shubhenduda and Henadi's simple, minimalist lifestyle was a model.

Shubhenduda's austerity also involved walking long distances and travelling by notoriously crowded Calcutta buses. He would never take a taxi even in the sultry heat of a Calcutta summer. Once, Tinni, who was in college then, was on a cycle-rickshaw when she saw her father walking along the pavement. She stopped and asked him to get on board. Dad said, 'Your father might be rich, mine wasn't,' and kept walking.

According to an apocryphal tale, Shubhenduda was asked by his boss in Sahitya Akademi, who was in Calcutta on an official visit, to carry his bag at the airport. Instead, Shubhenduda came home and sent his resignation letter. There may not be any truth in the story, but if it was indeed fabricated, it showed what perception people had about Shubhendu Sekhar.

At that time, he was in mid-fifties, with no sign of another job on the horizon. One day, I asked him tactlessly, 'How will you manage?'

He gave one of his mischievous smiles, 'Don't you worry! I am not going to touch you for a loan.'

At that time, the West Bengal government decided to bring out an edition of the complete works of Rabindranath Tagore. The Cultural Affairs Minister offered Shubhendu Sekhar the task of editing the volumes. He was given an office, an assistant, and two typewriters, but he refused to accept any remuneration, despite not having a steady income at the time. When I asked him why he wouldn't accept a fair compensation, he said, 'The day I accepted payment from the government, the babus would start kicking me around. I would much rather hold my head high and work for free.'

Towards the end, when his health was failing, he accepted a government vehicle. Shubhenduda passed away in 1993, by which time 15 of the 16 volumes of the complete works had been published. He died in the saddle at the age of 61. He was possibly one of the last specimens of humans that cares little for worldly comforts, but would die, if it came to that, to hold their head high. Everyone in his family, including his wife and daughter, called him Moni, which in Bangla means gem.

Rarely is a nickname more appropriate. He was one of the most pristine, pure, and coruscating gems I have come across.

48|Goodbye to a Girl on a Long Journey

I cannot recall her name, but I cannot forget her beautiful eyes with long eyelashes. Slender and beautiful, she was 15 or 16 when I met her, while I was a few years older. In another time, I could have easily fallen in love with her, but the question didn't arise because when we met, she was dying. I was in college then.

I loved our campus and I would often stay back in hostel during vacations. I spent those long peaceful days of solitude mostly at the university reading room, wading through printed pages usually of non-textbooks. I loved both the solitude of the deserted hostel, the library, the campus, and in particular, the company of Anuttam, the child of a broken family who had no home to go to during vacations. I will come back to Anuttam soon, but for now, let me get back to the story of the beautiful girl, which you must be dying to read.

The story began one afternoon during a summer vacation when I was in the reading room, which was not a room. It was actually a big hall with a high ceiling; comfortably cool; its large windows were covered from outside with thick mats of khaskhas reeds on which water was splashed from time to time. On the other side of the mats, the mid-summer heat was scorching. Most of my friends and my only girlfriend had gone home. I was as lonely as the searing wind howling on the barren field outside. There was not a soul on the roads.

That afternoon, I had an unexpected visitor in the shape of a profusely sweating stout young man around my age. He had come riding a bicycle from a village on the other side of the River Kopai, at least 15 kilometres away, in that sweltering heat. He was carrying a handwritten note from Tarapadada on a paper torn out of a notebook. With difficulty, I deciphered Tarapadada's terrible handwriting: "Gyan's sister has been ill for months. The local doctor can't figure out what her problem is. Can you take her to a good doctor in Calcutta?"

I hadn't met Gyan before. A farmer's son, he studied mathematics at Bolpur College. Tarapada—whose story I have told you—was a political activist on the other side of the law. He often stayed in Gyan's home in his itinerant life as a fugitive revolutionary; Gyan's family adored Tarapada.

A few days later, Gyan and I took his sister to Calcutta Medical College, the largest hospital and medical college in Calcutta then and now, situated on an enormous campus that stretched the distance between two major thoroughfares of the city—College Street and Central Avenue. The girl, who had never travelled beyond her village, looked at everything with a wide-eyed wonder, which made her beautiful eyes even more beautiful.

The doctor who saw her asked us to wait. Hours later, when almost everyone had left the OPD, he called us in and said the hospital would admit the girl as an in-patient for detailed investigation. Gyan and I looked at each other—we had very little cash on us because we hadn't expected anything beyond consulting a doctor. But it wasn't a problem: the treatment, accommodation, and food, everything would be free. No strings had to be pulled, and beyond the hospital ticket which I think cost 25 paise, nothing had to be spent. If you are familiar with the healthcare system in West Bengal today, i.e., in 2021, you may think this is a concocted story. But it is not. Gyan's sister got treatment under specialist physicians, and good care in a "general" ward for free.

Gyan visited the hospital every day; I accompanied him once or twice. We shared a room in our house and I gradually got to know a person who lived just 15 kilometres from my hostel, but in a different universe. Gyan had very little in his pocket. He would walk the distance of 10 kilometres to the hospital every afternoon. A week later, the doctors said his sister had been diagnosed with juvenile diabetes, a condition for which there was/is no cure. The only possible treatment, insulin injections on a continuing basis, was not feasible for someone from a remote village in West Bengal. For all practical purposes, it was a post-dated death certificate. She would be discharged the following day.

On the day of her discharge, Gyan's rubber slippers snapped. It was beyond repair. We spent some time to buy another pair from a roadside vendor. Gyan haggled energetically to get as good a bargain as he could. May not be because of this, but we were delayed. When we reached her ward, we found someone else in Gyan's sister's bed.

The duty nurse said after waiting for a long time, the hospital had transferred Gyan's sister to a home for destitute women. We should go to Building X, Ward Y, and meet Sister Z for more information. Our hearts sank.

In the labyrinth the Calcutta Medical College complex is, wards with their white beds, grey cabinets, and black oxygen cylinders fleeted past us as we ran along crowded passages, ashamed and angry with ourselves for being so utterly irresponsible. We went to one ward after another, only to be told that we should try "there".

Finally, we reached "there" and found her, sitting alone in a large empty room on an ornate chair. She was unbelievably calm, although her large eyes were brimming with tears, which began to flow freely when she saw her brother. For me, it was a moment of everlasting shame.

After spending the night at our home, when the three of us reached Bolpur railway station the following evening, the girl was in no condition to take a bus. As Gyan didn't have the cash needed to rent even the cheapest hotel room in town, I smuggled brother and sister into Dashachakra hostel. A mighty summer storm had just begun; the thunder storm, the downpour, and the concomitant power outage came as a big relief as there was no one to notice us.

I had taken a big risk; discovery of a girl in my room would have led to serious consequences for me, if not the end of my modest academic ambitions. But the summer vacation wasn't over and the 10 rooms of Dashachakra were empty except for Anuttam, who—as I have told you—had no home to go to. Anuttam and I chatted deep into the night, leaving my room to Gyan and his sister.

The following morning, Gyan took the first bus to his village leaving his sister behind. When it was dusk, he returned with a broad smile on his face sitting on a bullock cart with a semi-circular roof made of bamboo shavings.

After the previous night's storm and shower, the cloudless sky was exceptionally clear that evening. As we walked behind the bullock cart, we realised it was a full moon. As far as we could see, the undulating plains of Birbhum were washed by a soft but exceptionally bright moonlight. My watch showed eight, but in the sleeping villages around, it would have been beyond midnight. Television was in the womb of a distant future.

Anuttam, Gyan, and I walked along the uneven alleyway. A kerosene lantern was tied under the carriage of the cart. Working like a projector lamp, it threw long dark images of the wheels one moment, and at the next, as it swung the other way, the shadow became short. It was a mysterious light-and-shade show. None of us talked. Absolute stillness reigned, except for the monotonous grating of the bearing-less wooden wheels.

We didn't talk because each one of us was thinking—in our different ways—about the beautiful girl in a simple printed cotton sari sitting on the cart under its falcate roof, with her head tucked between her folded knees, a sculpture of the eternal helplessness.

After crossing Goalpara, we could see the River Kopai at a distance. Most of the year, Kopai has ankle deep waters. But that summer evening, she was a brimming wide stream of cold silver shining under a full moon. Anuttam began singing the timeless Manna Dey song, first in a murmur, and then gradually, he let his mellifluous voice fill the world.

> I'm the night, you're the moon
> Shining in the sky,
> Your image on my crystal mirror
> Is trembling, blushing shy.

We had planned to say goodbye to our guests from our side of the river. But Anuttam, immersed in his song, kept walking across the river following the bullock cart. Water rose almost to our chest and then fell. The song continued to overflow two sides of the river, spreading beyond horizons in the moonlight and adding another intriguing facet to the magical evening. As Anuttam sang, the thought crossed my mind that I had never experienced anything like that ever.

I was young then. I didn't know that such ethereal moments came but once in our lifetime if we were fortunate. "This world comes across her only once, never again."

On the other side of the river, we bade adieu to Gyan and his sister. Their destination wasn't far off, but soon, the girl would begin a far longer journey.

Postscript: the last page of the story has been torn away. I do not know what happened to Gyan's sister. But a week after this incident, police raided Gyan's house, looking for Tarapada Guha. Tarapada wasn't there; Gyan answered the door. A police officer reeking of liquor shot Gyan in his chest with a heavy, ordinance-factory-made revolver from a point-blank range. Gyan somehow survived, but I never met him again.

49|The Singer in the Stream

Now I am going to tell you the story of the singer in the moonlit river, Anuttam. He was special. His brother Gautam, a few years younger, too was a fine specimen of human being. The brothers would often sing aloud as happiness overflowed their merry souls. Neither of them would pick up a fight with anyone; they didn't have an enemy. Gautam, who would become a professor of philosophy at the Central University in Silchar, died young.

If I might take a short detour, among the Bengali singers of the 20th century, Debabrata Biswas (1911-80) stood alone. He began his musical journey with the Indian People's Theatre Association, an organisation allied to the Communist Party of India, but he is remembered as a singer of Rabindranath Tagore's songs. A self-taught musician, Debabrata was adoringly called George by his friends and fans. His big booming bass timbre, unadorned style, and warmth made him hugely popular and widely loved. On the other hand, George Biswas was reviled and harassed by the establishment that controlled recording of Tagore's songs after Tagore's passing. Here is my translation of a few lines from his autobiography in Bangla: *Brātyajoner Ruddhasangeet*[xxx] *(The Stalled Music of the Outcaste)*. It happened in the 1930s, during a winter fair in Santiniketan.

> Near the prayer hall, on one side of the gate was Kalo's Tea Stall…After hanging around in the fairground for some time, I would sit down at the stall. I didn't have to say anything. As soon as he saw me, Kalo smiled broadly and put a cup of steaming tea in front of me. He had reasons to smile; he knew what would follow. Tagore's granddaughter Buri (Nandita Kripalani) or someone else would spot me at his tea shop and announce to one and all: 'George has come! George has come!'

An impromptu musical would begin as Kalo's tea stall would get filled with familiar and unfamiliar faces in roughly three minutes. First, George would sing alone, and then in chorus. The space before the stall would be chock-a-block with his adoring listeners.

Anuttam Biswas was unrelated to George Biswas, and neither was he a bass. But his captivating baritone was equally treasured by his considerably large circle of friends and admirers. I believe if Anuttam hadn't completely lacked an ambition to strike it rich in the world, he would have become a famous singer. Those who had heard him sing once would fall in love with him. Much later, Anuttam and I joined a weekend trip to Digha with a large group of old friends, most of whom didn't know everyone in the group. The group included the former revolutionary Tarapada, his wife and their daughter. After the dinner one evening, we requested the hotel staff to give us the dining hall for half an hour.

With the sea rumbling in the background, songs flowed out of Anuttam like a cascading stream. People started pouring in and the dining hall got filled in no time. Hotel employees came and stood among the audience after their long day's work. The four doors of the dining hall were chock-a-block with enchanted listeners. After an hour, we wanted to stop, but the employees—who would sleep in the dining hall—insisted that the show go on. Anuttam kept the audience enthralled; not a pair of feet moved. The magical music ended in the small hours.

Anuttam was once admitted as an in-patient to Kolkata's PG Hospital for a heart condition. For a fortnight or so, he told tales, cracked jokes, played pranks, and made friends with fellow patients and the hospital staff. And he sang. I was not in Kolkata then. A common friend later told me that his ward had turned into a corner of bliss in the otherwise gloomy infirmary. The nurses fell so much in love with him that they cried the day he was discharged. Have you ever read a true story like this?

* * *

Anuttam had an unusual pet name, Bhondul, which means topsy-turvy in Bangla. Whoever named him Bhondul had great prescience. He did look at the world differently. He followed his own rules and perhaps had the insight to see how confused and upside down the real world was. Years later, I once spent a day at his home in a small market town in rural Bengal. Anuttam taught Bangla literature at the only college there.

Both Anuttam and his wife Sreela sang and we talked in between. After a while, the men felt a drop or two would make the evening even livelier. However, in that hypocritical small town, it was unthinkable that a college prof would buy drinks from the only liquor shop there in full public view. So? Anuttam told me, 'No problem, come with me.'

We walked through narrow lanes and crossed a permanent pontoon bridge as he took me along to the only bookshop there and, after handing over a small chit to its owner, Anuttam said, 'Please see if you can get this book.'

'Yes, Sir,' said the bookseller deferentially, 'of course.'

The name of the book was "A Large Bottle of Old Monk". It was faithfully delivered to the teacher's home a little later.

As I said in the last chapter, Anuttam had no home to go to during vacations. He used to stay in the hostel and eat wherever he could. We spent a lot of time together in Dashachakra, the hostel with ten rooms around a courtyard. Besides singing, he also wrote some of the most beautiful poems I have read in Bangla. Perhaps he got his literary genes from his maternal grandma, Ashalata Sinha, who had been one of the first Bengali women to have published a novel. The elderly lady used to visit our hostel from time to time. At that time she wore saffron. She had become Sanyasin Asha Puri.

Her older grandson too was weary of worldly attachments, although he was never on a religious path. Anuttam was a rare combination of an extrovert and a loner. The blend is not easy to handle, but he wore the conflicting hats effortlessly. At least once, the loner in him got the better of him—he ran away from home. He was travelling ticketless somewhere in North India when he was caught and sent to jail. From there, he sent a two-sentence postcard to his father, "I am fine. I am in jail."

As you would have noticed by now, Anuttam did not care to follow the familiar patterns of life. He was not someone who would send New-Year cards; he wouldn't or possibly couldn't keep in touch with friends. Neither am I good at it. So, from time to time, we lost touch completely for years together. But when we met, we picked up the thread as if we were meeting after a week. The last time, it was by pure chance.

My wife and I discovered him at a toy store in a shopping arcade in Kolkata. Anuttam had gone there to look for a particular board game for his grandson. He introduced us to the shopkeeper by his first name; the man seemed to be one of his old pals. Anuttam made friends easily.

Following the meeting, he and Sreela came home and we spent a glorious day together. It happened on 27 April 2015. I know because my phone, quite unemotionally, recorded the date when I took a few pictures. We parted with promises to meet soon and with lots of plans to spend time together… I couldn't imagine then that Anuttam would be diagnosed with brain tumour in 2016 and would be no more in another three years' time.

His death didn't bring tears to my eyes. His passing means that a very special kind of music has stopped forever. And I will have a void and a dull pain buried deep in some corner of my being for as long as I live.

If you were fortunate, you would meet someone like Anuttam only once in your life—never again.

50|A Railcoach in Darkness

That winter afternoon, the sky had decided to put on a special golden make-up. As the train was approaching Dhanbad, I stood at the door, soaking in the yellow landscape that I would later identify with a Van Gogh painting. The train was crossing a bridge over a road when I heard a loud noise. A piece of rock had hit our coach. As I looked below, I saw the two young men who had thrown the missile standing by a motorbike, laughing heartily. Welcome to Bihar, which was synonymous with lawlessness then. The state of Jharkhand was yet to be born.

At the Dhanbad station, I got off to check the damage. The rock had hit the coach about 10 inches from where my nut had been. there was a deep dent at the point of impact.

A little later, the train disgorged me at Kodarma, a tiny mining town in Bihar. As the train left slowly—almost with a touch of reluctance—the people who got off with me melted into the yellow wheat fields around. I stood on an empty uncovered platform under a dipping sun and a sparkling sky. There was a nip in the air; time hung lazily over the horizon like an invisible mist.

I was eighteen or nineteen then. From Kodarma, I would go to a remote place where my friend Animesh's parents and little sister lived, to spend my Christmas holiday. There was nothing there except a rail station, a few houses, a jungle around the hamlet, and a tiny stream. It was a remote outpost of the Indian Railways where my friend's dad was the station master. His station was tiny; just one passenger train stopped there in the morning and another in the opposite direction in the evening. In the late afternoon, a railway engine from Kodarma transported railwaymen who worked night-shifts at different stations along the route.

A solitary coalfired engine at one end of a platform was in fact ready to begin its journey. It had a narrow ledge by the side of the driver's cabin and behind it. Several men stood there holding on to shining brass handrails. As I looked at it, the rare prospect of travelling on a railway engine excited me no end.

However, the journey never happened. The engine driver had a message for me: 'Mitra Saab's little daughter took ill last night; she is in Dhanbad Railway Hospital now. The entire family is with her. Haven't you got the telegram?'

I stayed back at the Kodarma station, waiting for a return train which wasn't expected soon. Darkness descended quickly and an icy wind blowing in from the Himalayas forced me into the waiting room. As I settled down in a long reclining chair smelling of the British Raj, I watched darkness and absolute silence through window panes. I was the only living being around. The ancient, dimly lit waiting room began to tell her tales. The wristlets of a newly-wed girl jingling with dreams and anxiety … the utterly hopeless mute fear of a lost child … the happy footsteps of a husband coming home after years….

'Waiting for the train to Dhanbad?' A young man interrupted my musings.

'Yes, I am.'

'It's delayed. Not expected before eleven.'

The stranger, Dilip, was in his early twenties, with a slim athletic body and a weather-beaten unshaven face. He looked tired. With a warm smile, he introduced himself using an English word.

He said he was a "prospector", which was rather baffling. You didn't expect to meet a prospector at an Indian rail station in the second half of the 20th century. Those people—who often had mules to carry their luggage, wore Stetsons, and carried a gun—lived long ago in Africa, Australia, or California, didn't they? Weren't their stories told by Rider Haggard, Jack London, Charlie Chaplin, and our own Bibhuti Bhushan Bandyopadhyay? Dilip explained, he was into mica mining, which was, in a way, not very different from gambling. One had to take a tract of land on lease and start digging.

If fortune smiled on him, he would come across a large chunk of mica and become an instant millionaire. But millionaires are in short supply, most of them end up paupers. Dilip, a colliery owner's son, too had lost a large part of his inheritance in the quest, but was confident to hit the jackpot soon.

As we had our supper at a roadside eatery I noticed that Dilip was a frugal eater. We both were in that magic phase of life when people naturally trust others, when strangers can become friends in half an hour. By the time we finished supper, we had indeed become buddies. Dilip had lost his parents long ago, in a car crash near Hazaribagh, and had been brought up by his grandma.

When we returned to the station, it was dark outside; there was not another soul there. Back in the waiting room, both my new friend and I dozed off. After an indeterminable period of restful sleep, I was suddenly woken up by a big commotion. The deserted station had been filled chock-a-block by a boisterous crowd, mostly men. I thought I was dreaming; how did so many people materialise from nowhere?

The magical transformation had come about because a circus show had just ended nearby. These were the spectators on their way home.

When a passenger train arrived, a real-life circus began. The coaches were full and all the doors were secured. As it happens everywhere in India, the people on the train didn't care much for their less fortunate brethren outside. The doors remained tightly shut. The people on the platform banged doors, tried to prise open windows and made full use of their lung-power. Colourful vocabulary of Hindi swearwords flew at their charming best. Every time the train began to move, a young man would jump onto a buffer and pull a lever at the top end of the coach to stop the train. After several stops, a few doors were reluctantly opened and a surprisingly large number went in. Many others hung on to the foot-boards, ignoring the freezing gust of wind. The train chugged out.

Another train arrived and left in the same fashion, and most people managed to leave. I think, left to himself, Dilip too would have made it. But he didn't, out of sympathy for his newfound infirm friend. By then, the station had been enveloped in a dense fog and no other train was scheduled to stop that night.

If you think that that was the end of excitement for the night, you would be mistaken. A long goods train with maybe, 60 wagons came in and stopped on a track away from the platform. Seconds later, it began to move slowly. The harmless event produced a huge commotion at the station, with railwaymen coming out of their offices, shouting and gesticulating. The station's public address system was switched on at full volume and someone was desperately exhorting the driver and the guard of the goods train in Hindi, 'The signal is still red. Please stop and come back. Please, please! A mail train is coming on the same track. Aap rukhiye aur turant waspis aiye! Aap rukhiye aur turant waspis aiye!'

After some time, the train came back slowly with a touch of embarrassment. As it stopped, a totally sozzled man was taken off the engine and helped on to the platform.

The world was back to normal, dark, silent, and bitterly cold. And moments later, mail train with hundreds of sleeping men, women, and children went past the platform on the other side at a breakneck speed like a storm.

Dilip and I walked briskly on the platform to keep ourselves warm. Clattering teeth ruled out a chat. Despite being an agnostic from late childhood, I prayed to God for a minor miracle in the shape of a warm, empty train. Soon, God appeared from out of the fog in the figure of a railway porter wrapped in a ghostly blue blanket. Pointing at a rail coach in darkness some distance away on a sideline, he said that the dabba would be hitched to the first train leaving towards Dhanbad early next morning.

We thanked the porter God and ran along the railway line ignoring the irregular stone chips below. I climbed on to the pitch-dark dabba first, hoping to find an empty bunk on which I could stretch myself. But there was something on the way; I stumbled and fell headlong. I wasn't hurt because fortunately, I had fallen on something soft. I wondered what it could be.

Soon, the penny dropped. I was lying on a bunch of sleeping humans. The compartment was packed like a tin of sardines. There was not an inch of vacant space; the air was thick with the bidi smoke and snoring. But no one minded the intrusion. Sleeping bodies were moved willingly to make room, and somehow, room was made.

When I woke up, it was morning. The board on the platform read Dhanbad. Dilip had left.

51|Sunrise from the Tiger Hill

We don't have a nook of golden bloom
Or an alley hidden in forest gloom.
Swiftly in the evening draught
A nameless flower spreads its waft,
On arrogant branches, says the bard,
Rhododendrons, with scant regard,
They glance happily right through
The golden rays in the morning blue.[xxxi]
– Rabindranath Tagore

Like lots of literate Bengalis from the plains who had never seen rhododendrons, I had an emotional connection with the flower through these lines of Rabindranath Tagore.

I got to see the flower when I visited Darjeeling on a college excursion. In the nippy November air of the stunning hill station, rhododendrons were in full bloom. The first thought that came to my mind on seeing the flower was that, for once, one couldn't accuse Tagore of poetic excesses. A large flower in different shades of red and pink, rhododendrons, unlike most flowers, don't look delicate. There is something bold, beautiful, and arrogant about them. They seemed to be wild flowers that had deigned to be around in a human habitation. As incongruous as an eagle in an aviary.

As we got off at the tiny Darjeeling rail station, we were in the middle of a quaint small town where people, dogs, and homes looked very different from what I had seen. Houses and stores—they were all made of wood—were mostly one-storey. Most homes had potted plants in front of them. Mongrels had shaggy hair; men and women were strongly built and fair-skinned. Older people had deep furrows on their faces. If there hadn't been packets of Surf detergent and

Parle biscuits in shop windows, I could have imagined I was in another country. (I hadn't been to any other hill town in India, if I had, I would have known that they look somewhat similar, from Shimla to Shillong.)

At the heart of Darjeeling is an open public space, the Mall, where men with ponies were pestering tourists for a short ride and photo opportunity. Assessing our financial worth quickly with their experienced eyes, they left us alone. We drifted from one point to another and some of us took black-and-white pictures with our inexpensive cameras and expensive 120 mm films which had just 12 frames on a roll. As he was taking a picture of a bear in the zoo, a friend, Animesh said to his subject, 'Son! Give me a smile.' Instead of smiling, the bear pounced at us within its cage. One can understand why celebrities cannot stand the paparazzi.

We visited a century-old eatery called Glenary's which sold fabulous cakes. It was a two-story restaurant with large glass panelled windows. We would spend a long time with a coffee there when our legs got tired.

We stayed at a place called the Shailabas which was a few hundred feet above the town. After a day of fun and frolic, we would wearily trudge the last stretch of the ascent, panting, eager to get under the four blankets allotted to each of us. There was no heating—nights were frigid.

The day before we were to return, we planned to visit the Tiger Hill to see the sunrise—a mandatory touristy thing to do. We had to start early in the morning, maybe, around four thirty. The place was 11 kilometres away, near Ghoom. At 8,500 feet it was the highest peak in the Darjeeling district, if I am not mistaken; we had to go uphill along a road which only jeeps could negotiate, after engaging their front-wheel gears on some stretches.

We had organised seven jeeps for all of us. Six of them arrived on time. When we enquired about the seventh, the drivers who had come were evasive. No assurances, no excuses. It was too late (rather, too early) to get another vehicle.

A few of us self-appointed "leaders" had to pay the price of our vanity. While the rest of the group left, we stayed back. Cursing the unknown driver and shivering in the freezing cold, we looked out from under the hotel portico, eager to catch a glimpse of two dots of light on the winding road below. There were none. Minutes trickled to an hour. The only bright spot in the dismal story was that Amitavada, a few years my senior, had very thoughtfully saved a flask of brandy for such contingencies. We took swigs in turn, and soon stopped feeling the chill.

When the jeep finally arrived, it had been clearly too late. A stout Ghurkha staggered out from behind the wheels. Thoroughly sozzled and reeking of country liquor, he could barely stand.

We, particularly I, did what no sane person would do with a thoroughly drunk Gurkha who possibly carried the mandatory kukri. But stupidity, thy name is youth. Made worse by the brandy, I guess. We showered the man with the choicest abuses, that too in our terrible Hindi. His eyes blazed in fury, but he said calmly, 'Tumko sunrise dekhna hai? Dikha denge.' Period.

When the jeep hit the road, we realised our folly, but it was too late. Our driver was not only drunk and furious, but also mad. The sharply winding, steeply ascending road had a precipitous chasm on the right. The man behind the wheel didn't look ahead, never;

instead, he put his nut out of the window on the right and looked below. Watching the edge of the road with his possibly bleary eyes, he drove at full throttle. Icy wind rushed in through the open window and the gaps in the tarpaulin cover, hitting us like shrapnel. Time and again, the jeep came precariously close to the edge and screeched to change direction. We knew we would not only see no sunrise at the Tiger Hill, but nowhere else either. Never ever.

Perhaps there is indeed something called Fate. And that morning, she decided that I should write this story decades later. When we arrived at the Tiger Hill observation terrace after covering the distance in about a fourth of the normal time, it was still dark. The terrace was a big semi-circular green patch with a railing. Flat as a tabletop.

As we trained our eyes towards the east, darkness was reluctantly making way for light. But nothing much had changed. Someone tapped me and said, 'Look back.'

On turning back, what I saw was worth dying for. The western sky had horizontal bands of myriad colours: violet, indigo, blue, … was the sky working like a gigantic prism that split the seven colours of the light from the rising sun?

The mighty Himalaya was waking up on yet another day, like he had done for millions of years. The Kanchenjunga caught fire with the first rays of the sun. There was no mist. We could see the Everest far behind. In a few moments, countless peaks of the Himalayas started glittering in their primeval glory. The mighty mountain range stood before us in silent grandeur.

There are a few things that you must experience if your life is to be complete. Sunrise over the Tiger Hill in a clear morning is one of them.

52|Raghupati Raghava

[While the rest of this book contains true stories, maybe garnished a bit for effect, all the characters here and in the next story are imaginary. Any coincidence with anyone alive, dead, or in coma would be purely coincidental.]

During the many years I've been writing my stories, I have rarely written about an unpleasant event or individual. It isn't surprising because memory has a self-cleansing facility: it removes disagreeable experiences from one's hard disc. Yet, some special people defy the built-in software of your brain and stay on, by the sheer strength of their character. Raghupati Banerjee, Raghu to his countless friends and admirers, is one such. Raghu, a colourful fellow with many qualities, was my classmate in college. I haven't come across many people who are more capable. Or more complex.

I haven't met Raghu in decades, but I've heard from common friends about his spectacular success in construction business in India, Bangladesh, and Sri Lanka. And although he has made billions, he's the same down-to-earth Raghu of the olden days. The door of his palatial building in Kolkata—I am told—is open to friends at all times. His many friends from the country who visit the city on various errands stay in his house for as long as they wish to. Raghu doesn't have the time to meet them often, but he has never been stingy in his hospitality.

Incidentally, I spotted Raghu's business acumen early; I knew he would make it big. How did I know? I'll tell you in a moment, but before that, here's a sketch of Raghu's personality. He was warm, charming, intelligent, and a compulsive liar. He could light up any gathering of friends with his earthy humour and ribald jokes. It was always great to have the ever-smiling and sharp-witted Raghu around. But behind the happy-go-lucky exterior, he had a mind of steel. Unknown to the rest of the world, he was a local leader of the Communist Party of India (Marxist Leninist), CPIML for short, commonly known and usually dreaded as Naxalites.

In the course of the present narrative, I have touched upon the Naxalite movement, but let me get back to it quickly for the sake of the story I am telling you now. There were several groups of Naxalites who worked independently and sometimes, antagonistically, but the CPI ML was by far the dominant group for which violence was the central creed. Their supreme leader Charu Majumdar—as we have seen—figured that the easiest way to fix inequality, injustice, and all social pathology to bring in a perfect classless society would be to kill "class enemies". They called the murders they committed "annihilation" (of class enemies). Their targets were mainly exploitative landlords, moneylenders, and traffic constables.

Once, in a bitterly cold winter morning when we returned from a college excursion to Ghatshila on the banks of the Subarnarekha, we heard Dr Radha Mohan Sinha had been "annihilated". The elderly physician Radha Mohan was rich, but he didn't satisfy the other qualifications to be annihilated. He was popular in our small town and was known to be a generous man who helped the poor. During the trip, Raghu had been with us and regaled us with his jokes. Much later, we would come to know that he was the mastermind behind the murder of Dr Sinha. He had gone on the excursion to have a watertight alibi.

His luck however ran out after some time. He was arrested and tortured in the police station. After a few months, he was released on bail shortly before our final exams. Although he hadn't had the requisite attendance, the university allowed Raghu to take the final year exams "on compassionate grounds".

This happened during a summer vacation when I was in Calcutta. Raghupati telephoned me and said somewhat abruptly, 'Do you know what you should do when the police beat you?'

'I've never had the good fortune.'

'Keep this in mind. When they thrash you, you should cry out as loudly as you can: "Bābāre, māre, more gelumre!" or anything else, but you must holler as loudly as you can.'

'How does it help?'

'It makes your pain less unbearable.'

Raghu didn't call me with the altruistic motive to train me about how to deal with police torture, which in any case wasn't an impossibility for boys of my age in Bengal those days. He wanted me to help him out with preparations for the forthcoming exams.

It was decided I would return to hostel, where he would join me. With nobody else around, we both would prepare for the exam in the solitude of an empty hostel. I too thought it would be a good idea. Besides, I was exceedingly fond of Raghu. The prospect of spending time with him was not a minor attraction.

On the appointed day, there was no Raghu. His family—they lived in a small market town in a neighbouring district—was well-off, but those days, personal telephones were rare. There was no way I could get in touch with him.

After waiting alone for two days in a building with 79 empty rooms, I became a little worried about my friend. Had he been picked up again? So, I took a train and then a bus to where Raghu lived. Although I had no idea where his house was, given his fame, I could easily find out his digs.

Well, digs wouldn't be the right word to describe a huge two-storey brick-and-mortar building with the usual embellishment of blue lotuses (or maybe, pink flying geese) on the parapets of balconies. The gate, solid, black, and enormous and no calling bell. (Did Raghu's old man too fear annihilation by Naxalites?) After I made sufficient noise, a naked man in just a loincloth showed up from behind the narrowly opened gate. When I asked for Raghu, he said curtly, 'Raghu Babu isn't home.'

'Where is he?' 'Gone to attend a wedding.' 'Where?' 'Don't know.' 'When will he be back?' 'Don't know, …'

I returned to hostel and spent the rest of the holiday alone, having food from a roadside eatery.

Keeping people waiting was Raghu's speciality. Years later, he called me up in Calcutta one evening. I was working for a law firm then. Raghu wanted to discuss some legal issues relating to his business. There was a sense of urgency in his voice when he said, 'I must talk to you face to face. Are you home?'

He hung up after saying he would be there in an hour. I expected him not to come, an expectation he fulfilled. But Days later, he did come to my office. That was the last we met.

At that time, Raghu had been in business for many years and had breached the commercial threshold of his tiny hometown; he was a civil contractor and a well-known businessman in his district and beyond. He had his ways of dealing with government officials. For example, according an apocryphal tale, once he bought a second-hand car, got it refurbished, and drove it to the wedding reception of a local PWD (Public Works Department) engineer's daughter. While leaving, he left the keys and papers of the vehicle with the official as a wedding gift and got home by rickshaw. He rose spectacularly, specialising in bridges and water tanks.

However, among his many hits, there were a few misses, naturally. A recently built bridge on the river Kopai collapsed, killing a number of people. The local people were furious and wanted to lynch the contractor, that is, our man Raghu. The powers-that-be quickly arrested him and kept him in safe custody for months. By then, Raghu had come a long way from his revolutionary past. He had joined the ranks of dodgy small-time businessmen who are an integral part of the power structure in Indian small towns. He had moved to the other side of the power equation, from left to right.

53| Raghupati Shows an Early Spark

While introducing Raghu, I said I would tell you how I knew—pretty early in his career—that he would make it big. To explain, I'll have to take you back to a time when we were doing Masters. Raghu had been in and out of jail since our failed rendezvous before the final exams. The Naxalite rebellion was failing spectacularly; their leader, Charu Majumdar had died in police custody on 28 July 1972 after being the state government's guest of for 12 days. Raghu had also fallen in love with a bright, beautiful girl, Neera, a few years our junior. (Neera would go on to do PhD and become a physics prof.)

We had a brutal government in West Bengal then, which handled Naxalites in four different ways.

The first group was killed by police or their hired goons in cold blood or otherwise. There's no official estimate about the number, but it's widely believed around 5,000 young men and women, including some of the finest of our generation, were killed.

The second group, to which belonged a majority of the Naxalite activists, often suffered torture in jail and managed to destroy—wholly or partly—their future. After a point, they drifted away from the self-annihilating movement and found various ways to deal with life. Later, police harassed some of them by foisting criminal cases, and sometimes, forced them to work as spies or informers. As the stories of these unfortunate souls aren't glamorous, their sacrifices have been unrecorded and largely forgotten.

A third, much smaller group, the offspring of people with power and deep pockets, were bundled off to Europe or North America for higher studies and rehabilitation.

The last group was encouraged to set up businesses locally and given financial support like seed capital and bank loans.

Raghu belonged to the fourth set.

Raghu's story began with a college excursion and it will end with another. On our annual excursion, we went to Darjeeling that year, our second trip after the watching the memorable *Sunrise from the Tiger Hill.* Raghu wasn't with us. He had left both studies and revolution and begun small-time civil contract work in his hometown. But he would often visit our campus on his super-noisy Enfield 350, primarily to catch up with his girlfriend.

The journey is more exciting than the destination. The saying is true for the 70-kilometre train ride from Jalpaiguri to Darjeeling, which the tiny, narrow-gauge *toy trains* covered at a leisurely pace in four to five hours. The beautiful blue train had only three coaches with big windows without iron gratings. It would move slowly, particularly while going uphill. There was a bitumen road by the side, almost all along the railway track. Getting off and on the running train was fun.

As normal brakes wouldn't work on steep inclines, there was another toothy rail in the middle, parallel to the principal rails. If for some reason the train had to be stopped on an ascent or descent, the engine driver would lower a gear which would catch the toothy rail.

When the gear was jammed in addition to usual brakes, the train couldn't but stop. Also, for some reason, not one, but three trains would leave the New Jalpaiguri station one after the other keeping a distance of a few hundred metres between two trains.

I stood at a door on the second train as it was climbing a particularly steep incline. We crossed one of the many picturesque rivulets on the way, along a jangling bridge with no parapet. I looked at the stream far below, from the banks of which children waved at us wildly. The winter sun was dipping on the horizon and the Himalayas looked gorgeous in the orange glow of the setting sun. The ancient train was chugging on a steep ascent.

Suddenly hearing some noise, I looked ahead. The train in front was rolling back uncontrolled, gaining speed every moment. The engine driver was shouting and gesticulating madly to the driver of our train. After a minute or so, our driver stopped and started reversing. I jumped off and saw the third train had stopped on the rickety bridge we had just crossed, a few hundred metres away. If the third train remained stationary, our train would crash on it right on the bridge without a superstructure, with unimaginable consequences. The people who had got off our train started shouting to the passengers who hadn't, asking them to jump off.

Soon, people started jumping off our train. Some managed neatly, but many jumped in the wrong direction. I saw human bodies dropping like sacks of potatoes. The budding physicists of our group had no such problem, but two girls had nasty falls because they were wearing sari. One of them was Neera, Raghu's lady love.

I do not remember how our group completed the journey, but I didn't, that day. Neera and Pranati both had head injuries; were taken to the nearest hospital in Kalimpong in hastily arranged taxis. The hospital admitted them. As someone had to be around to look after the injured girls and to deal with emergencies, I stayed back in Kalimpong until their parents arrived two days later. Fortunately, they were safe by then, each with dozens of stitches on their heads.

* * *

The down Darjeeling Mail reached the Bolpur station early in the morning a week after the accident. Near the exit, I saw a beaming Raghu, a little late as usual, but eager to meet Neera. Clearly—in a world with only a few largely inaccessible telephones—he hadn't got the bad news. I took him to a tea stall and broke the news gently.

Dumbfounded, Raghu looked at me for a long time through the steam over our teacups. The silence, which was beginning to be a little uncomfortable, was broken by a deeply reflective Raghu, speaking more to himself than to me, 'I am getting some tarpaulin sheets at a throwaway price. I don't need them right now, but should I buy them for the future?'

It was my turn to be dumbfounded. After hearing that Neera was safe, the calculating soul in Raghupati Banerjee—unknown to me till that moment—had turned completely towards worldly affairs. In a few minutes, he asked me to join him as a business partner. I said, 'Raghu, you won't find a more useless partner.'

'I know, but you can speak and write English.'

Therefore, I got the first job offer in my life thanks to the pernicious long-term aftereffects of British colonialism. I asked him, 'After working so long for emancipation of the poor, how do you find it when you yourself have to exploit workers?'

'You're dead wrong. In business, you can make money without exploiting anyone.'

'Really? How?'

'My first contract was to construct a road in my hometown. Underneath the surface, I had to put first quality bricks. Instead I just put third-quality bricks. … And made a huge profit without exploiting anyone. Do you get the point?'

I knew Raghu had a bright future.

54| Reinventing the Memories of Anup

It was during the winter vacation. While returning from somewhere to our university township one evening, I had to change bus at Keernahar, a tiny market-town in Birbhum. When I reached there, the last bus had left.

Small market towns in rural Bengal (or perhaps in rural areas anywhere in our country) have something forlorn about them. By the time I reached the place, darkness and dew were descending on the almost empty bus stand, that is, an old brick-and-mortar shed which had been taken over by beggars and vagabonds after dusk. Some of them were fast asleep. The bus station also had a few small eateries and stores selling biscuits, cigarettes, torch cells, and other life-saving products.

There were only a few people around, and the shops were shutting down. Soon, the crepuscular darkness turned the place into a black-and-white watercolour painting when a few dim Edison-era yellow electric bulbs were turned on here and there. The storekeepers and the passengers from the last buses, who were getting away briskly, were clearly getting ready for sleep, but the marketplace had been sleeping already. It was a page from a Shirshendu Mukhopadhyay story that was yet to be written.

As I was drinking my super-sweet milky tea sitting on a bench made of bamboo staves, a gust of freezing wind blew in from Darjeeling. I realised that my light cardigan was no match for the icy Birbhum winter night. I also had nowhere to go.

There were no hotels in such tiny places in the Bengal countryside. In such a situation, the standard operating procedure was that stranded travellers would spend the night sleeping on a tea-shop bench. However, the easy camaraderie that had been a part of rural Bengal was coming to an end in the early 1970s. Earlier, people would gladly let in a stranger and allow him to spend the night on their outer veranda, if not in the home itself. But in the time I am talking about, before wheedling a free lodging for the night at a rural tea shop, one had to establish that he was neither a thief, nor a Naxalite running away from police. I guess I didn't have the sharp features of a professional thief, but given my age, I was a high-risk candidate of the second category.

I suddenly recalled that a boy two years our junior at university lived in Keernahar. I didn't know him well then. But I asked the owner of the tea stall if he knew Anup Kumar Roy who studied at …. The shopkeeper, who was very unlike the usually talkative Bengalis, just grunted. I took another glass of tea and tried to imagine what the next 10 hours would be like. In about 10 minutes, Anup appeared, picked up my bag and said simply, 'Come, Santanuda.'

It seemed someone had overheard me enquiring about Anup, and given the proximity of people in our villages and small towns, the message had reached him in minutes.

It was the beginning of a deep friendship. Anup took me to his home which was a very old and large red-brick building. It would have been built by a wealthy zamindar long ago. By then, the mansion had been partitioned into a few independent dwelling units—which too were huge—and Anup's family lived in one of them.

Anup was a strong student. After graduation, he went to Calcutta University to do Masters in electronics. Then he began working for the Electronic Corporation of India, a company known to people for their sturdy black-and-white TV sets in those days.

By then, I too had been posted in Calcutta and Anup, a bachelor then, was one of the regulars in the set of close friends who would often gather in our flat in the city. We discussed and solved all the problems of the world and spent glorious weekends together. The most significant difference between then and now is that the future didn't look so dismal those days. We had dreams in our eyes.

Sadly, my peripatetic profession took me away soon and I lost touch with Anup. Many years later, we briefly met at the Dum Dum Airport. I was about to board my first flight to Canada (in fact, my first outside India), and Anup was there to receive his wife, who had been living in the US. That was 25 years ago. We never met again.

I don't know why I thought of Anup this morning. Memory plays queer tricks on us, doesn't she?

55| An Airhostess among Mendicant Musicians

Dhriti, who enrolled in a Master's programme at our university, had been an airhostess in her previous birth. And she did look like an ex-airhostess—tall, slim, and gorgeous. As far as dress sense went, Dhriti was roughly two generations ahead of her time. She was often seen in economical shorts and spaghetti tops, not to mention faded jeans and see-through shirts.

Soon, she formed an apparently deep friendship with her classmate Keshav, who we called Keshavda because he was a married man in his late-forties. The liaison disappointed many, needless to say. Keshav, was short, dark, and fat, but had an intelligent face with a bushy beard and piercing eyes. The last object, behind a pair of circular metal-rimmed glasses, made him look like a nineteenth-century Bengali intellectual who had just materialised from a Rabindranath Tagore novel. He wore parachute pyjamas and white often-unwashed kurtas. When Keshav and Dhriti were together, aesthetically and sartorially, they were a study in contrasts. The odd pair was always seen together, on the campus and off it. Actually, they were a threesome; they had a sidekick too, a thin guy of vague features. But lackeys are not remembered by history, not even as footnotes. I've forgotten his name.

Keshav was a touch snooty; normally, he wouldn't deign to talk to lesser mortals like yours truly although we were in the same wing of our hostel building. The first time when I had the good fortune was an evening when both of us happened to be customers at Raju's hooch shop in Goalpara. In winter, Raju sold excellent tāṛi made of date palm sap at his dimly lit open-air tavern where customer sat down on the ground in a circle. When we both were sufficiently tipsy, Keshav spoke to me at length. He was an erudite man. The light friendship we developed that evening when we were drunk continued in times when we were sober, unlike what had happened to Chaplin in *City Lights.*

I don't recall who was with me that evening in Raju's watering hole, but I clearly remember that Ganesh, a rikshaw puller I knew, was a fellow drinker that evening. I remember Ganesh's presence because suddenly, he burst out singing a familiar Tagore song, *Badal baul bajay re ektaara.* Bauls are a sect of wandering mendicant musicians in Bengal, who earn their living by singing on the roadside, near temples, at fairs, etc.; Ganesh's song was about a baul cloud playing a one-stringed instrument, as the matted hair of the sky darkened the world at the onset of a storm. The song was a tad incongruous under a cloudless winter sky lit up by a trillion stars above and a hurricane lantern below, but Ganesh sang it beautifully. His diction was rustic, but the tune was perfect. It was one of those unforgettable snippets of time that remains with you for ever.

A few months after the Goalpara meeting, my friend D and I were on a bus on our way to Jaydev Kenduli on the bank of the river Ajay. The local people believe—without evidence—that the village Jaydev Kenduli is the birthplace of the thirteenth-century poet Jaydev, who composed Geet Govinda in Sanskrit, a watershed on the Bengal literary landscape.

Jaydev Kenduli is also a religious centre with old temples and several ashrams where thousands of bauls congregate in the month of Poush (December-January), at the end of which a fair is organised over three days. The fair is actually a carnival of bauls, and it was also believed the best of Indian hemp was found there in happy abundance.

D, my partner in minor crimes, was a wonderful company. He had interest in almost everything in life and was a great speaker. (He is very much alive today. The past tense just indicates I've lost touch with him!) He and I wanted to get a taste of baul songs at their authentic best. We also looked forward to smoking grass.

As it was the last day of the fair, we just about managed to find seats on the last row of a public bus, which filled quickly. Soon, before us stood a solid wall of human bodies, all male, some of whom were smoking. Because of a freezing draft, the windows had been shut. The cocktail of smoke and human smell created an interesting ambience.

About half an hour into the journey, I had nodded off when there was a sudden commotion. It seemed everyone was jumping towards the front and left of the bus. Fortunately, any force applied within a moving bus doesn't have an impact on the bus as a whole, thanks to what Sir Isaac Newton had called his *Third Law of Motion.* Otherwise, the bus would have surely overturned. What was the matter, had a pickpocket been caught? When I asked a man in front, the excited man replied in the local dialect, 'Oh Dear! That female is smoking!'

D and I wanted to get to the bottom of the matter. As we stood up and craned our necks, we saw that the troika mentioned at the beginning of this story had seated themselves on the corner seat by the side of the driver. And Dhriti, in faded jeans and a white shirt, was calmly smoking a biṛi, the indigenous cigarette made of unprocessed tobacco and leaves. She was gracefully unaware of the commotion her simple indulgence in a minor pleasure had created.

Incidentally, that was the last time I saw Dhriti. She would leave our university a few days later, never to return.

* * *

Darkness descended soon after we walked from the bus stop to the river bank. Ajoy is a mighty river during the rains, but in the winter, water was nowhere more than waist-deep. The wide expanse of sand with a few slender streams were waiting for the holy dip to be taken by a few thousand faithful a few hours later. In the tenebrous twilight on the fairground dotted with trees, shacks, and small eateries, there were thousands of people. All of them except a few like us were children of Rural Bengal. And there was something else.

As I grew up in post-Partition West Bengal through years of refugees, floods, and droughts, I thought I had seen poverty, but that evening I realised I hadn't. Everywhere in the fairground, there were shallow holes of, say, six feet by two feet, crudely dug and covered with hay, twigs, and leaves. I had seen nothing of its kind before, and at first, I couldn't understand what purpose they might serve. The penny dropped after a while. They were temporary homes, not of the bauls, who stayed at the ashrams, but of beggars, who had gathered there in hundreds hoping to cash on the pilgrimage-induced generosity of the people taking the holy dip. In the biting cold of the Birbhum riverbank in mid-January, they had made for themselves the most wretched homes one could imagine. They were a sad side-story in the carnival of music.

The soul of the fair was in the many circles formed by bauls in colourful clothes, who were singing with the accompaniment of an instrument with just one or two strings, and sometimes, keeping the beat by holding their ghungoors in hand. Except for the singer, others were smoking grass from earthen pipes, which were passed on to the next person after a l-o-o-o-ng, unhurried puff. The pipe went around; the air was heavy with the captivating aroma of hemp.

After walking aimlessly for a few hours, when D and I were tired, we sat down in one of the circles and received the smoky prasad when our turn came, no questions asked. We listened to songs by rustic voices that recreated the smell of the Bengal earth and sky. In the dark new-moon night, anything outside that circle of holy bliss meant nothing. Gradually, the world beyond receded from our consciousness. Ecstasy!

The singers were poor men rich in happiness. The exact opposite of the money-rich-time-poor young urban professionals of our time among whom the divorce rate may be as high as one in three. The night grew older, but nobody noticed.

56| House No. 386

In a new, unfamiliar city, I have just moved into a house in a beautiful street smelling of childhood.

You'll find such an alley in every traditional old Indian city or town, from Kolkata to Vijayawada to Moradabad, but not in planned urban spaces, like say, Chandigarh or Durgapur. To give you a picture of the town where my new home is, residential buildings are closely packed here along the road. They are mostly small, not taller than three storeys, and no two of them look alike. Some houses have big ornate gates painted bright yellow, some have unpretentious small doors that haven't smelt of new paint for decades, and some have a small open space in front, with a cluster of trees bearing family history, under which a red cemented slab invites people to sit down and chat. Elsewhere, old, dimly lit stores stand as the façade for houses behind. I am tempted to peep into a store and check what they sell, but I don't.

My house has a red wooden door pushed back by a few feet from the road. I climb a short flight of stairs to reach a landing to unlock the main door with a large, ornamental key. The paint on the door is old, peeled off at places; it's a kind of entrance that makes you feel comfortable about the home behind. A horseshoe, which people connect to good luck, has been nailed on the door at the eye level. Just below are three more wrought iron pieces reading 3, 8, and 6. The house just before mine is numbered 385, but for some reason, the one that follows is marked 392. That is the house with a large yellow gate.

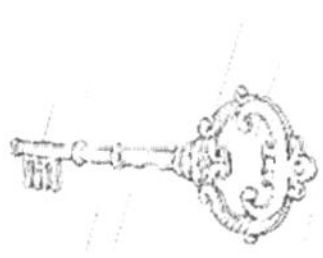

I keep my light suitcase and duffel bag in the first room, open windows to drive away the musty smell, and come out to explore my new neighbourhood. But as it often happens, the place has just turned into a college hostel. My house is a room now; 386 is my room number. I realise why the street reminded me of my childhood.

I walk past a white wall and a long row of doors, all painted dull grey. Towards the end of the corridor, as expected, I find the common bathroom for the floor, without a gender sign. I go in.

Filth accumulated since God-knows-when assails me. The baths on one side have broken doors, leaking showers, and thick layers of fungi on floors and walls. The toilets are overflowing, with an avalanche of putrid brown slithering towards me, slowly, but relentlessly. I am reminded of Mohammed Hanif's *A Case of Exploding Mangoes.* If you've read the book, you would recall the horrifying experience of Ali Shigri, who was held captive in an indescribably filthy windowless toilet for days.

However, I am more fortunate, I don't live in Pakistan. I turn around and run. Nobody stops me; I am back in the familiar, quaint road, and I hold the large key tightly for my dear life.

I walk on ... But I can't find my house. I go past the now familiar road a number of times. Every other structure is in place, but I can't find a door marked 386. Between 385 and 392, there is a wide alleyway washed by the morning sun, with blades of grass glistening with dewdrops. Was that how the other houses too vanished earlier? It doesn't matter though. Here I stand in my new city, with an ornate key in hand, but no door which it opens.

For the first time in my life, I realise how it feels to be homeless in one's own country.

Acknowledgements

My dysfunctional memory might prevent me from recording the names of everyone who helped me and contributed to this memoir indirectly. Apologies to those I am missing out.

Let me begin with my older sister Ruby who left us a few months ago. She had a major—though unobtrusive—role in many of the anecdotes in this memoir. She read the draft and corrected a few points. Ruby would have been delighted to see this book in print.

Besides her, I have picked the brains of my childhood friends Apurba Kundu, Debashish Sarbadhikari, Jyoti Prasad Chakraborty, Rajat Roy, Sanat Banerjee, and Swapan Chatterjee. Also, I could write about Pandit Dhrubatara Joshi thanks to Suktara Ganguli. Apart from them, I must acknowledge my debt of gratitude to many others.

In my extended family: Aditi Niyogi Poddar, Amit Biswas, Arindam Pal, Avik Sinha, Jana Palova, Monica Pal, Oindrilla Hazra, Pratikshadutta Niyogi, Rahul Chaudhuri, and most importantly, Tapan Biswas.

Friends who I have walked a long way with: Animesh Mitra, Asit Ghosh, Bratin Chatterjee, Chitrita Bhatacharya, Dipankar Saha, Kumar Dutta, Kumkum Mukhopadhyay, Nivedita Bardhan, PC Thomas, Paulose Varghese, Philip Abraham, Rahul Bhattacharyya Shibaditya and Shantabhanu Sen, Saswati Ray Chaudhuri, Satyajit Mitra, Somdatta Sinha, Subroto Hajra, Sumanto Ghatak, Sunil Mukherjee, and Bhawani Cheerath. During the many years this book has been on the anvil, Shibaditya, Kumkum, Subroto, and Sunil have left us.

Friends I met later: Brayan Beaton, Debarati Roy, Debasis Ganguli, James Bradbury, Koushik Chatterjee, Manab Chakrabarti,

Radhakrishnan Nair, Ranajit Chatterjee, Somesh Chatterjee, and my senior friend Nirmal Kanti Bhattacharjee. A special word of thanks goes to my friend and former colleague Chitra Nair, who not only encouraged me to write the memoir, but also said an unbroken mirror too could leave behind fragments!

Friends I have met on the social media alone: Beena Vijayalakshmy, Bernadette Carri-Dease, Mani Menon, Premraj Cheekoth, and Utsab Ray.

I am deeply indebted to Mohan Sivanand, an artist and a former Editor-in-Chief, Reader's Digest, India. Apart from writing a beautiful foreword for this book, he has also checked a number of chapters thoroughly and refined them to a large measure.

Since they arrived in the lives of my wife Arundhati and me, our children Sohini, Ritwik, and daughter-in-law Moumita have been sources of strength in whatever I've done. Arundhati has helped as captive reader and a robust critic of my writing. Pallak Gupte, another daughter to me, has contributed with her insightful views. So have my close friends, Gautam Ganguli and Swapna Chaudhuri. They gave me confidence with their generous, if indulgent, appreciation. KT Rajagopalan, George Thomas, and Basu Bhattacharya have been sources of inspiration for me for decades. Rajagopalan and George also checked the final proof for this book. I wouldn't try to thank them or the others I've just mentioned.

A big thank you to the young artist Amit Saha who has found the time to illustrate this book despite his pressing professional obligations. Readers would know what value he has added.

Finally, a few words about my friend Damodar (Damu) Menon. We didn't know each other then, but we lived nearby in Calcutta as children. He has been the touchstone on which I often checked the authenticity of some of my childhood memories. Besides, Damu has spent much time to check this manuscript meticulously and suggested many a change to make it better. If this book is not replete with factual or stylistic errors, much of the credit must go to him.

Endnotes

---

[i] Mihir Sengupta in *Bisahdbriksha / A Tree of Sadness*, (Subarnarekha, Kolkata, 2005) p12 © Baidehi Sengupta [Translation mine]

[ii] Kallol Lahiri in *Indubalar Bhater Hotel / Indubala's Lunchroom*, (Suprakash, Kolkata, 2020) pp57-58 © Author [Translation mine]

[iii] William Dalrymple in *City of Djinns*, (Bloomsbury 2017) p 61 © Author

[iv] Mohonlal Gangopadhyay in *Dakshiner Baranda / The Veranda on the South* (Signet Press Kolkata 2013) pp206-10 [Translation mine]

[v] Yuval Noah Harari in *Sapiens – A Brief History of Humankind*, (Penguin Random House, UK) pp398-99 © Author

[vi] Geoffrey Moorhouse in the introduction to his book *Calcutta* (Penguin Books, 1974) p13 © Author

[vii] Kriahna Dutta in *Calcutta: A Cultural and Literary History* (Roli Books, 2003) p171 © Author

[viii] Santosh Rabna in *Rajneetir Ek Jeeban / A Life in Politics* (Ananda Publishers, 2018) p94 [Translation mine]

[ix] James Bradbury in his essay *Refugee Megacity* – 14 September, 2020 https://www.synaps.network/post/india-bengal-kolkata-refugees-bjp

[x] Ramchandra Guha in *India after Gandhi* (Pan Macmillan Limited, 2008) p91 © Author

[xi] Krishna Dutta in *Calcutta: A Cultural and Literary History* – (Roli Books, 2003) p 31

[xii] Sandip Bandyopadhyay in *Ranakshetra Rajpath / Battleground Street* (Progressive Publishers, Kolkata) p17 [Translation mine]

[xiii] Sunil Gangopadhyay, *Chhobir Deshe, Kobitar Deshe / The Land of Paintings and Poetry* (Ananda Publishers Private Limited, Kolkata, First Edition, 2002) p10; © Author [Translation mine]

[xiv] Ruskin Bond, *Lone Fox Dancing – My Autobiography* (Speaking Tiger Publishing Private Limited, 2017) pp 7-8; © Author, 2017

[xv] Sunil Gangopadhyay, *Ardhek Jeebon / Half a Life* (Ananda Publishers Private Limited, Kolkata, First Edition, 2002) p186; © Author [Translation mine]

[xvi] James Hilton in *Lost Horizon*

[xvii] Oscar Wilde in *The Picture of Dorian Gray*

[xviii] Tapan Raychaudhuri in *The World in Our Time* (HarperCollins Publishers India, 2011) pp90-91 © Author

[xix] Stephen Hawking in *Brief Answers to the Big Questions* (John Murray (Publishers), London, 2018) p201 © SpaceTime Publications Limited 2018

[xx] Sir Ken Robinson in a TED Talk: https://www.youtube.com/watch?v=wX78iKhInsc accessed on 20 June 2021

[xxi] José Saramago, *Blindness* (Penguin Random House, UK, Vintage 2017 Edition) p127 © José Saramago and Editorial Caminho 1995; Translation © Professor Juan Sager 1997

[xxii] Rabindra Kumar Dasgupta in his *Collection of Essays, Prabandha Sangraha.* (Ebong Mushaera, 2007) p 117; [Translation mine]

[xxiii] Satyajit Ray in the preface to his memoir *Jakhan Chhoto Chhilam / When I was a child* [Translation mine]

[xxiv] Rabindranath Tagore, *Geetabitan* (Visva-Bharati Publication Department) Baishakh 1397 (April-May, 1990), p601 [Translation mine]

[xxv] Truman Capote in *Breakfast at Tiffany's*

[xxvi] Sunanda Sikdar in *Dayamayir Katha/Dayamaee's Tales* (Gangchil, Kolkata, 2010) pp 64-65 [Translation mine]

[xxvii] *Evaluators for preserving flawless answer sheets* – Neha Miglani in The Times of India. Archived from the original on 27 September 2016. Retrieved 28 February 2015

[xxviii] https://powerdriveblog.wordpress.com/2017/09/19/rabindranath-tagores-humber/ accessed on 04 August 2021; © Joydip Sur

[xxix] Somendranath Bandyopadhyay in *Shilpi Ramkinkar Alapchari / Artist Ramkinkar, in Conversation,* (Dey's Publishing, Kolkata (2019) p173 © Soumitro Bandyopadhyay) [Translation mine]

[xxx] Debabrata Biswas in his autobiography, *Brātya Janer Ruddha Sangit (The Stalled Music of an Outcaste),* Karuna Prakashani, 1st Edition, pp 58-59 [Translation mine]

[xxxi] From *Sesher Kobita, The Endgame of Poetry,* a novel by Rabindranath Tagore [Translation mine]